DYNAMITE ENTERTAINMENT PROUDLY PRESENTS

CHARLAINE HARRIS

GRAVE SIGHT

BOOK ONE

DYNAMITE ENTERTAINMENT PROUDLY PRESENTS

CHARLAINE HARRIS
GRAVE SIGHT
BOOK ONE

written by CHARLAINE HARRIS & WILLIAM HARMS

art by DENIS MEDRI

colors by PAOLO FRANCESCUTTO Gotem Studio

letters by BILL TORTOLINI

cover A by BENOIT SPRINGER (50%)

cover B by DENIS MEDRI (50%)

contributing editor RICH YOUNG

consultation ERNST DABEL & LES DABEL

special thanks to JOSHUA BILMES

cover A

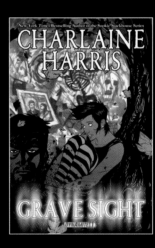

cover B

ISBN10: 1-60690-229-6
ISBN13: 978-1-60690-229-5

10 9 8 7 6 5 4 3

Dynamite Entertainment:

NICK BARRUCCI · PRESIDENT
JUAN COLLADO · CHIEF OPERATING OFFICER
JOSEPH RYBANDT · EDITOR
JOSH JOHNSON · CREATIVE DIRECTOR
RICH YOUNG · BUSINESS DEVELOPMENT
JASON ULLMEYER · SENIOR DESIGNER
JOSH JOHNSON · TRAFFIC COORDINATOR
CHRIS CANIANO · PRODUCTION ASSISTANT

WWW.DYNAMITE.NET

CHAPTER ONE

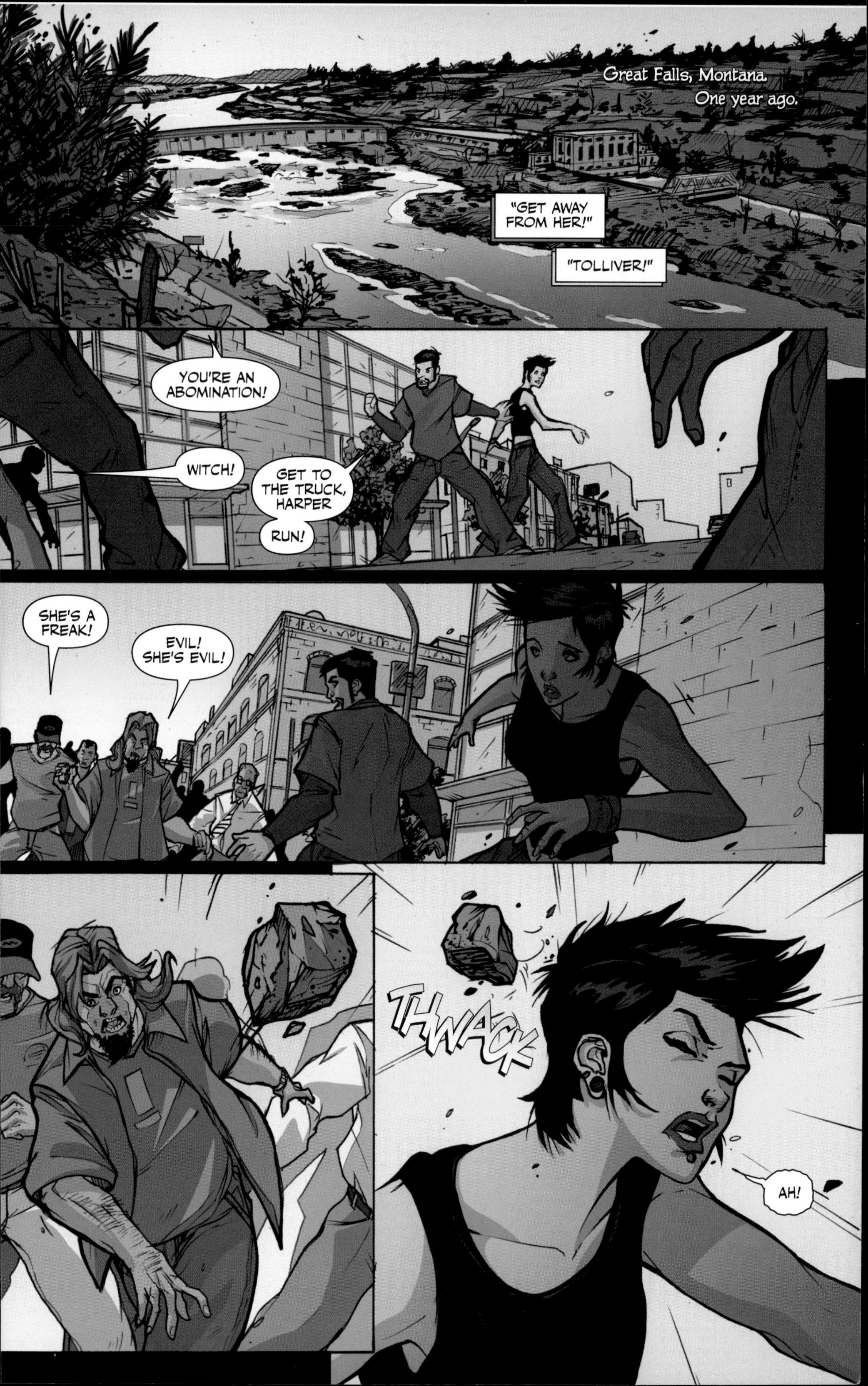
Great Falls, Montana.
One year ago.
"GET AWAY FROM HER!"
"TOLLIVER!"
YOU'RE AN ABOMINATION!
WITCH!
GET TO THE TRUCK, HARPER
RUN!
SHE'S A FREAK!
EVIL! SHE'S EVIL!
THWACK
AH!

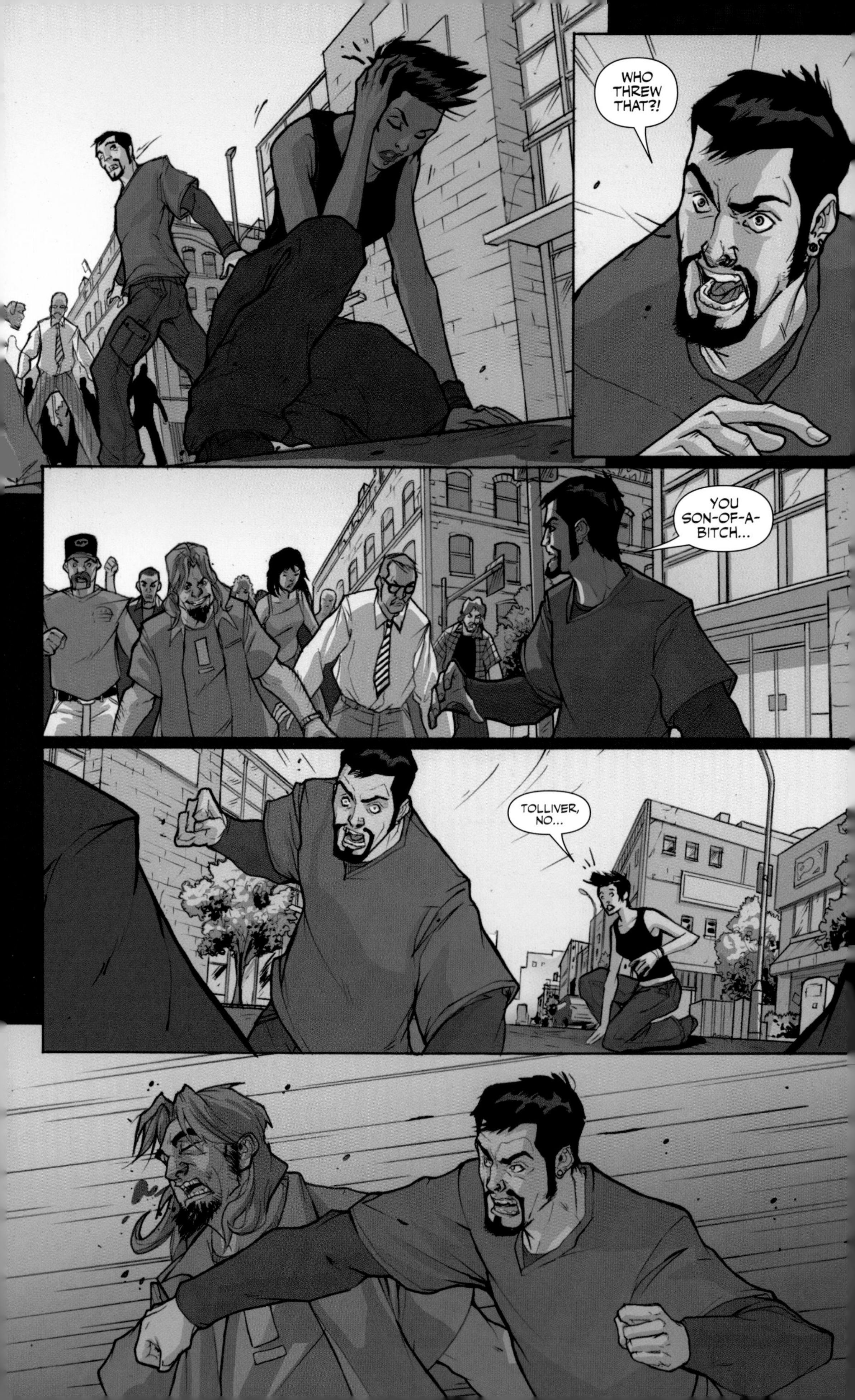
WHO THREW THAT?!
YOU SON-OF-A-BITCH...
TOLLIVER, NO...

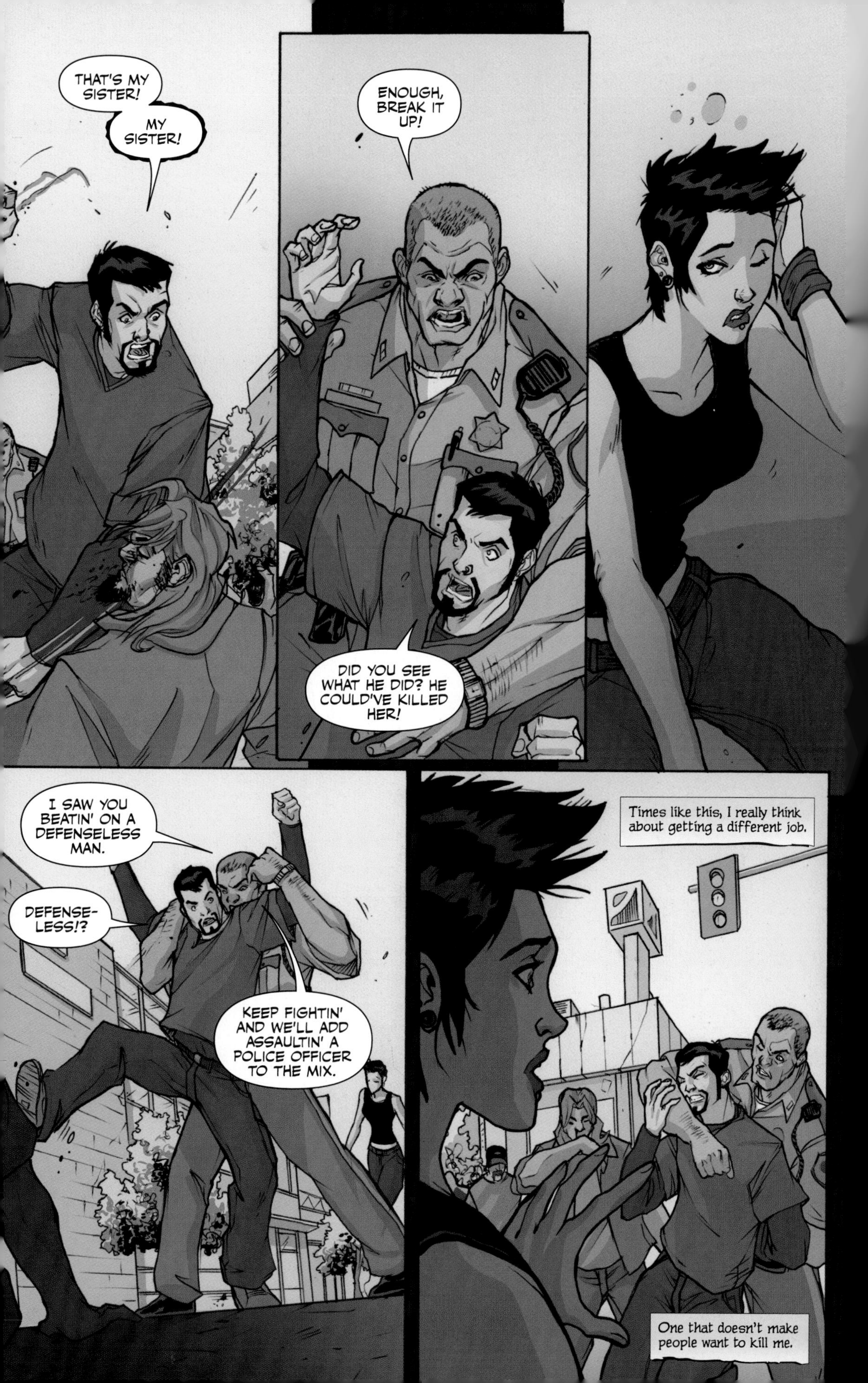
THAT'S MY SISTER!
MY SISTER!
ENOUGH, BREAK IT UP!
DID YOU SEE WHAT HE DID? HE COULD'VE KILLED HER!
I SAW YOU BEATIN' ON A DEFENSELESS MAN.
DEFENSE-LESS!?
KEEP FIGHTIN' AND WE'LL ADD ASSAULTIN' A POLICE OFFICER TO THE MIX.
Times like this, I really think about getting a different job.
One that doesn't make people want to kill me.

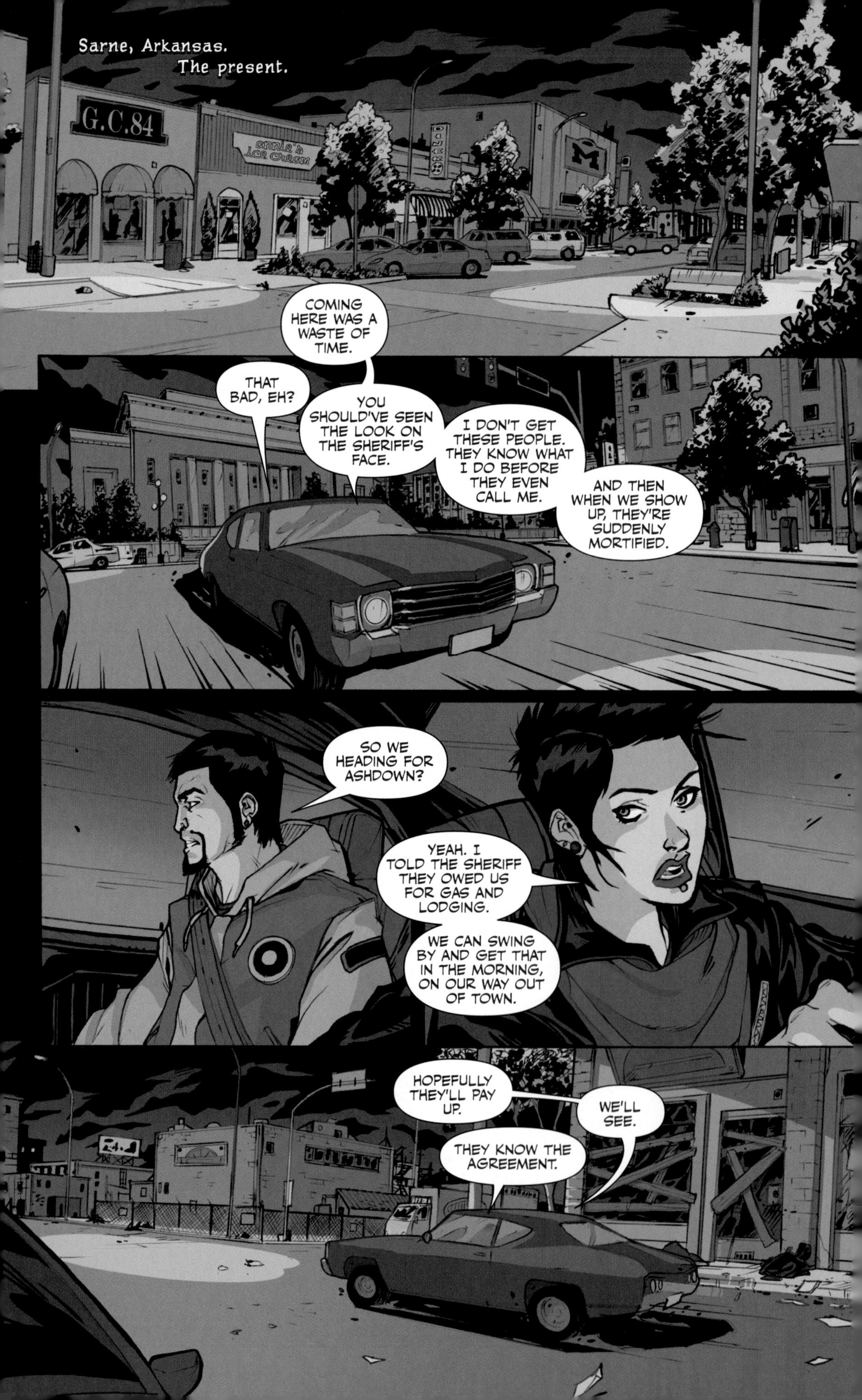
Sarne, Arkansas. The present.
G.C.84
annie's ice cream
COMING HERE WAS A WASTE OF TIME.
THAT BAD, EH?
YOU SHOULD'VE SEEN THE LOOK ON THE SHERIFF'S FACE.
I DON'T GET THESE PEOPLE. THEY KNOW WHAT I DO BEFORE THEY EVEN CALL ME.
AND THEN WHEN WE SHOW UP, THEY'RE SUDDENLY MORTIFIED.
SO WE HEADING FOR ASHDOWN?
YEAH. I TOLD THE SHERIFF THEY OWED US FOR GAS AND LODGING.
WE CAN SWING BY AND GET THAT IN THE MORNING, ON OUR WAY OUT OF TOWN.
HOPEFULLY THEY'LL PAY UP.
WE'LL SEE.
THEY KNOW THE AGREEMENT.

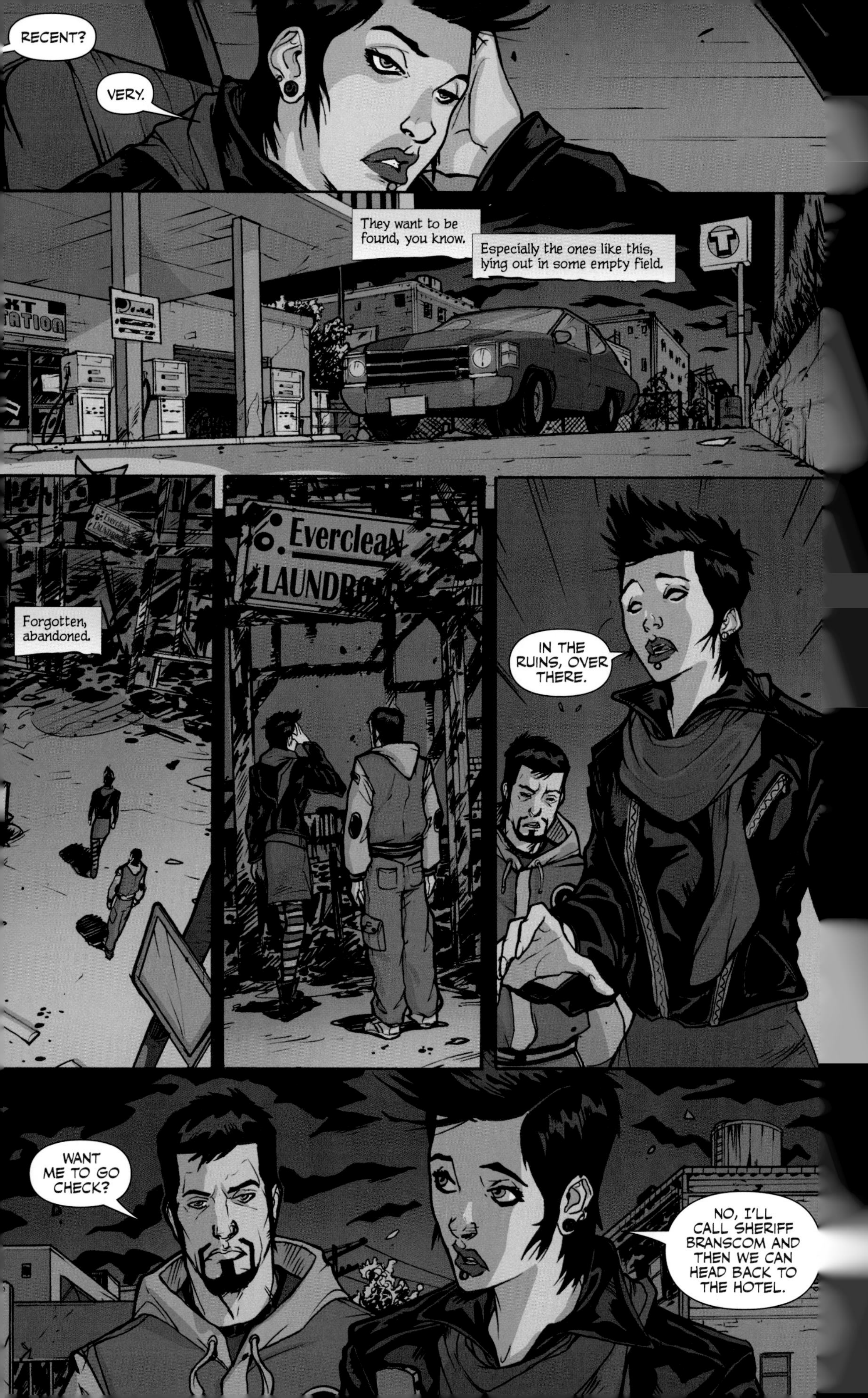
RECENT?
VERY.
They want to be found, you know.
Especially the ones like this, lying out in some empty field.
Forgotten, abandoned.
Everclean LAUNDR
IN THE RUINS, OVER THERE.
WANT ME TO GO CHECK?
NO, I'LL CALL SHERIFF BRANSCOM AND THEN WE CAN HEAD BACK TO THE HOTEL.

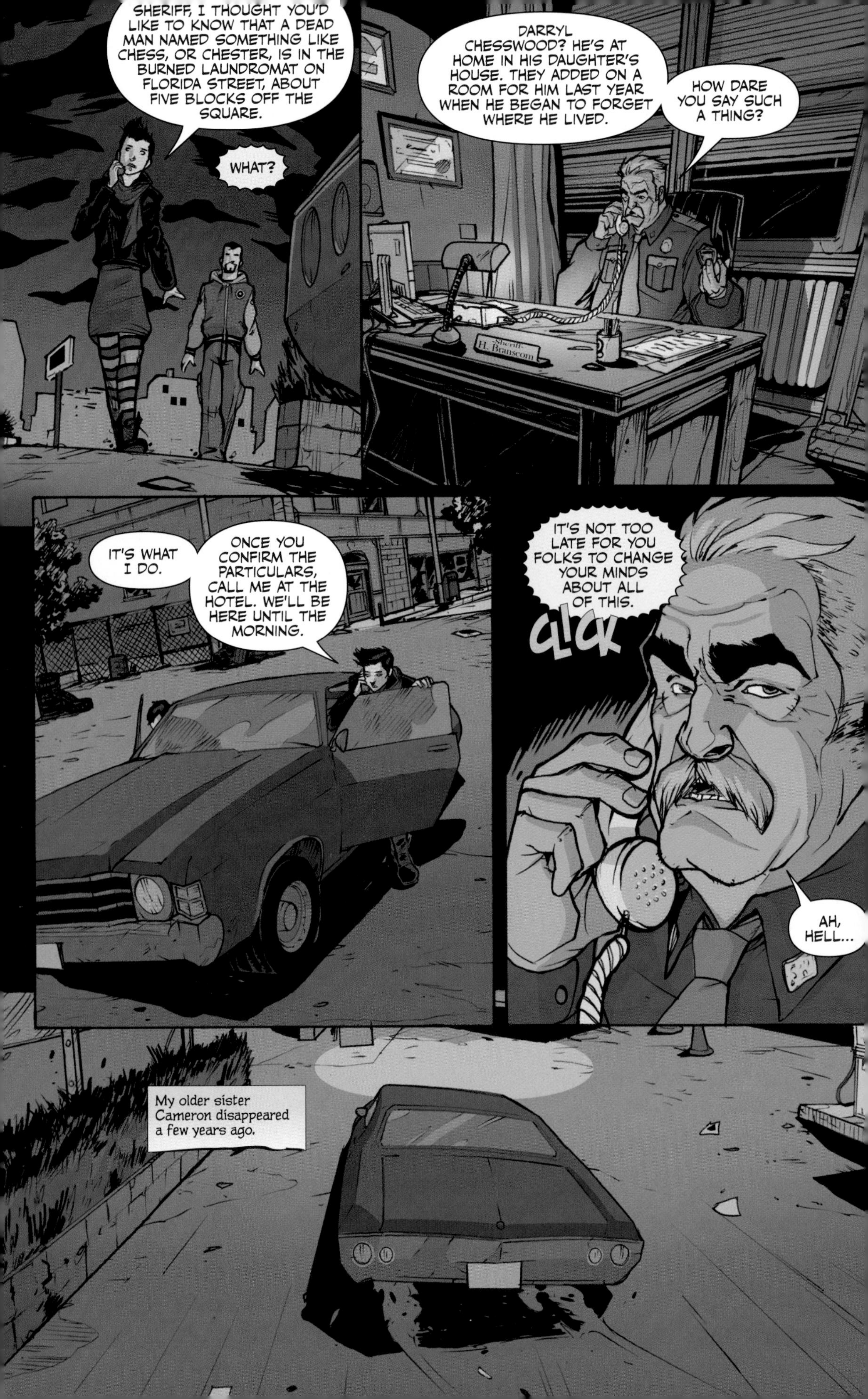
SHERIFF, I THOUGHT YOU'D LIKE TO KNOW THAT A DEAD MAN NAMED SOMETHING LIKE CHESS, OR CHESTER, IS IN THE BURNED LAUNDROMAT ON FLORIDA STREET, ABOUT FIVE BLOCKS OFF THE SQUARE.
WHAT?
DARRYL CHESSWOOD? HE'S AT HOME IN HIS DAUGHTER'S HOUSE. THEY ADDED ON A ROOM FOR HIM LAST YEAR WHEN HE BEGAN TO FORGET WHERE HE LIVED.
HOW DARE YOU SAY SUCH A THING?
-Sheriff- H. Branscom
IT'S WHAT I DO.
ONCE YOU CONFIRM THE PARTICULARS, CALL ME AT THE HOTEL. WE'LL BE HERE UNTIL THE MORNING.
IT'S NOT TOO LATE FOR YOU FOLKS TO CHANGE YOUR MINDS ABOUT ALL OF THIS.
CLICK
AH, HELL...
My older sister Cameron disappeared a few years ago.

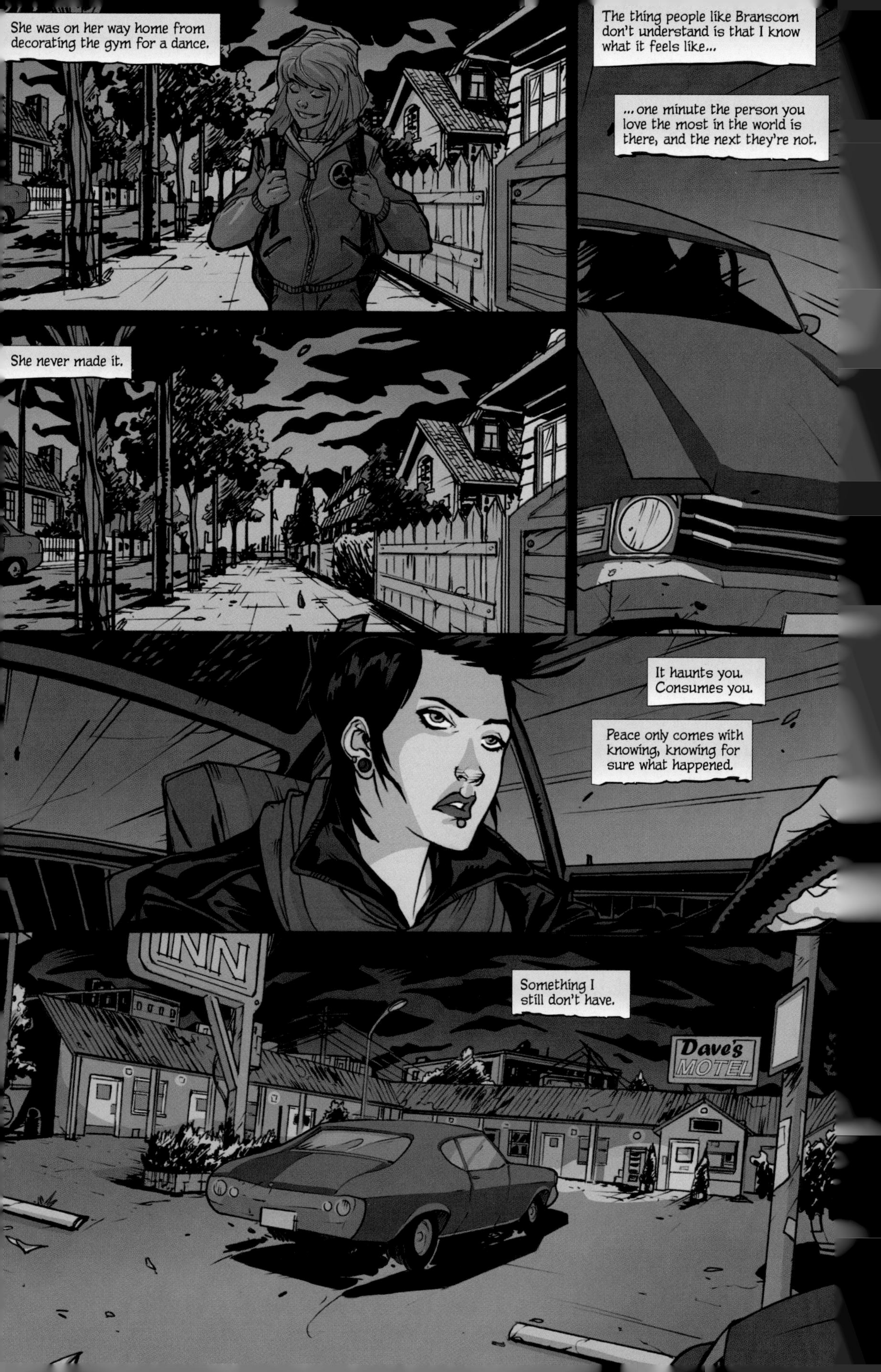
She was on her way home from decorating the gym for a dance.
The thing people like Branscom don't understand is that I know what it feels like...
...one minute the person you love the most in the world is there, and the next they're not.
She never made it.
It haunts you. Consumes you.
Peace only comes with knowing, knowing for sure what happened.
INN
Something I still don't have.
Dave's MOTEL

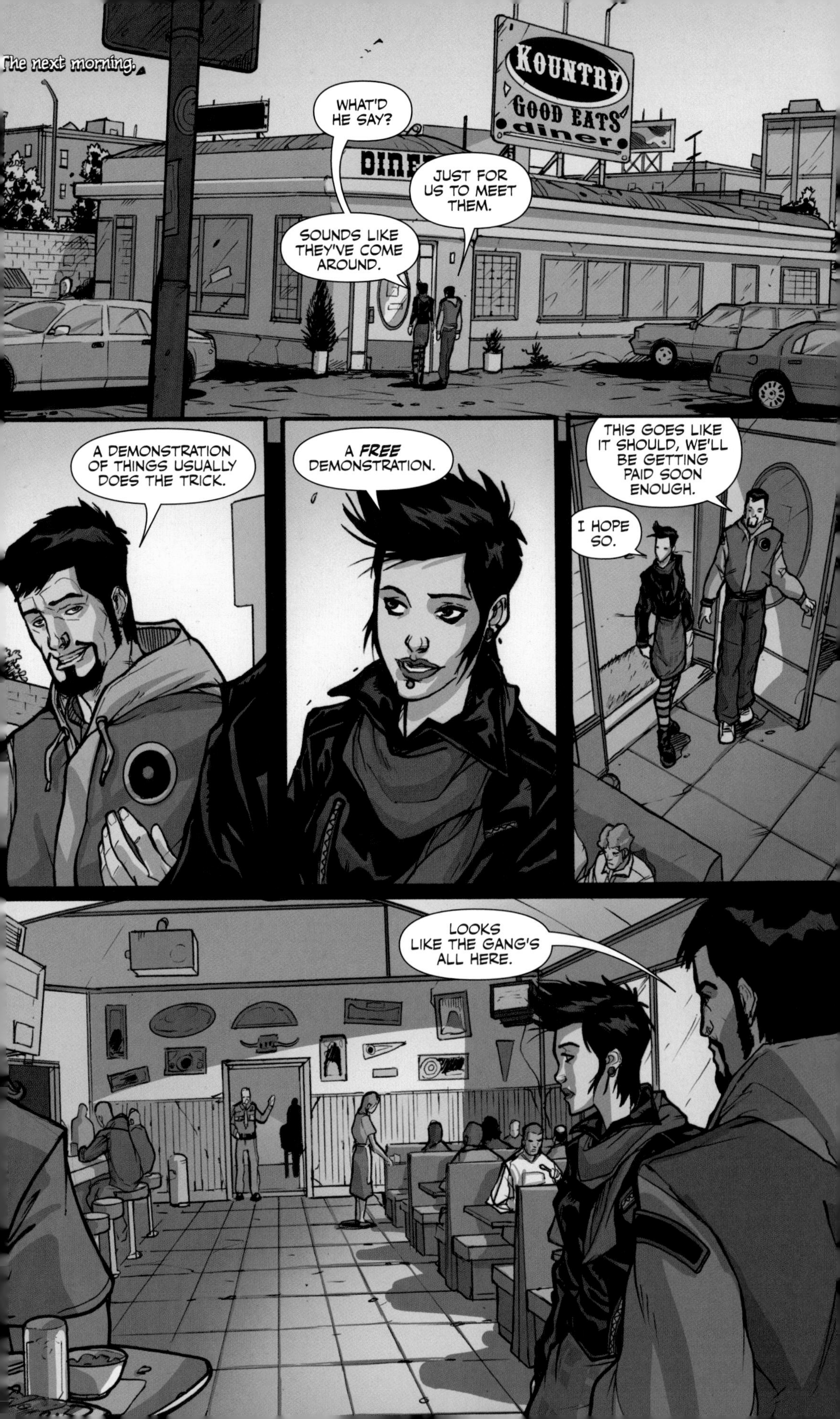

The next morning.
KOUNTRY
GOOD EATS
diner
DINER
WHAT'D HE SAY?
SOUNDS LIKE THEY'VE COME AROUND.
JUST FOR US TO MEET THEM.
A DEMONSTRATION OF THINGS USUALLY DOES THE TRICK.
A *FREE* DEMONSTRATION.
THIS GOES LIKE IT SHOULD, WE'LL BE GETTING PAID SOON ENOUGH.
I HOPE SO.
LOOKS LIKE THE GANG'S ALL HERE.

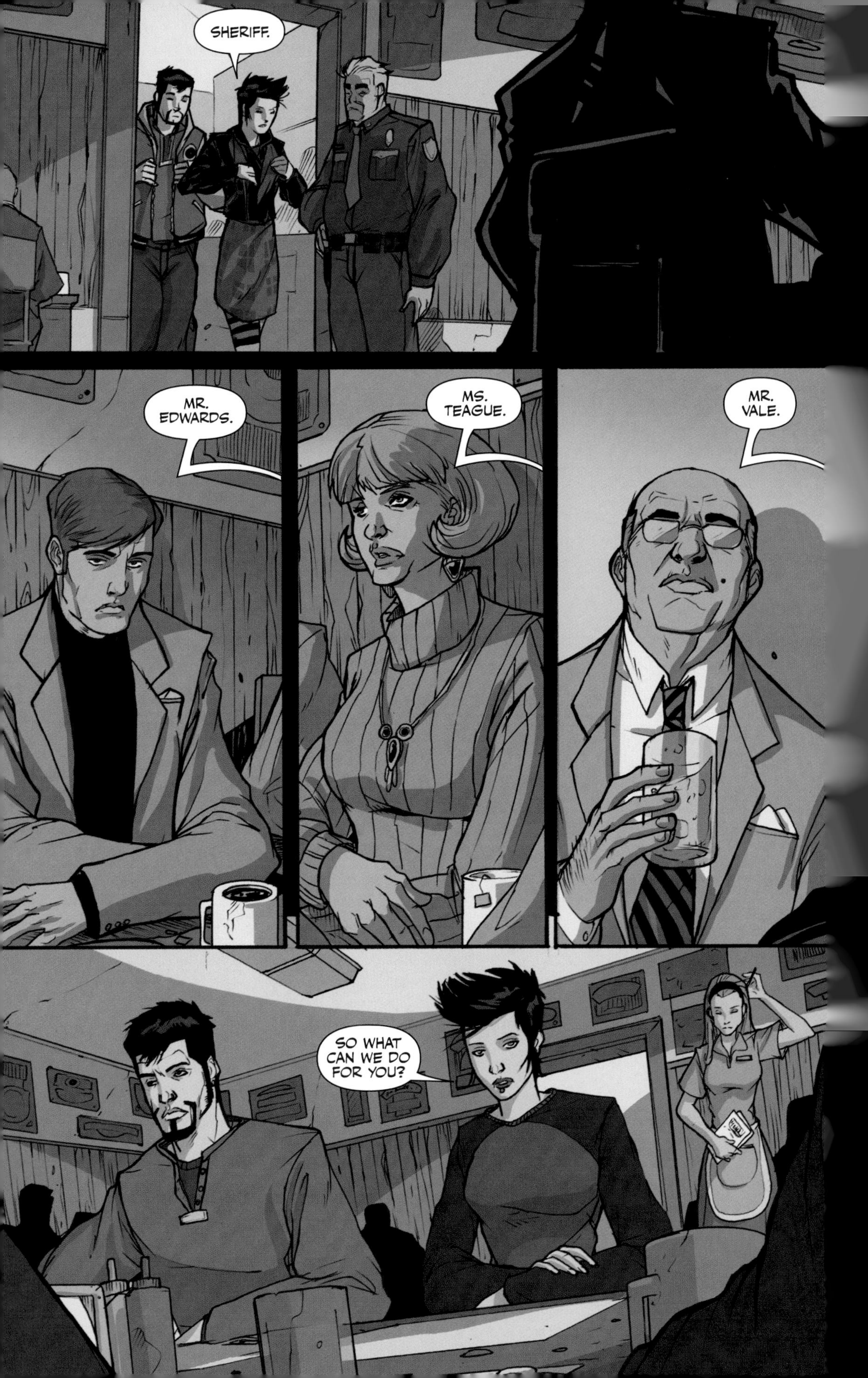
SHERIFF.
MR. EDWARDS.
MS. TEAGUE.
MR. VALE.
SO WHAT CAN WE DO FOR YOU?

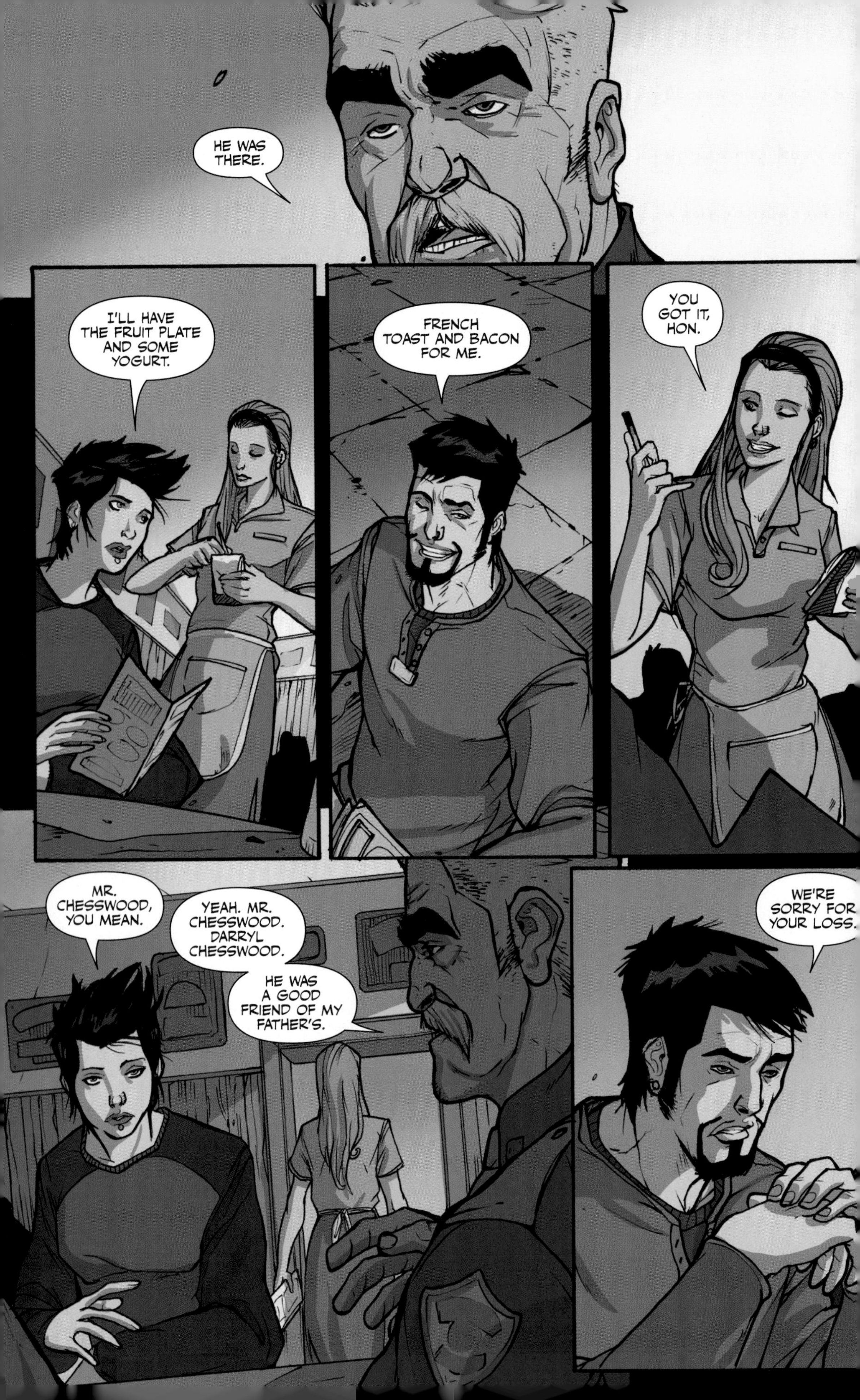
HE WAS THERE.
I'LL HAVE THE FRUIT PLATE AND SOME YOGURT.
FRENCH TOAST AND BACON FOR ME.
YOU GOT IT, HON.
MR. CHESSWOOD, YOU MEAN.
YEAH. MR. CHESSWOOD. DARRYL CHESSWOOD.
HE WAS A GOOD FRIEND OF MY FATHER'S.
WE'RE SORRY FOR YOUR LOSS.

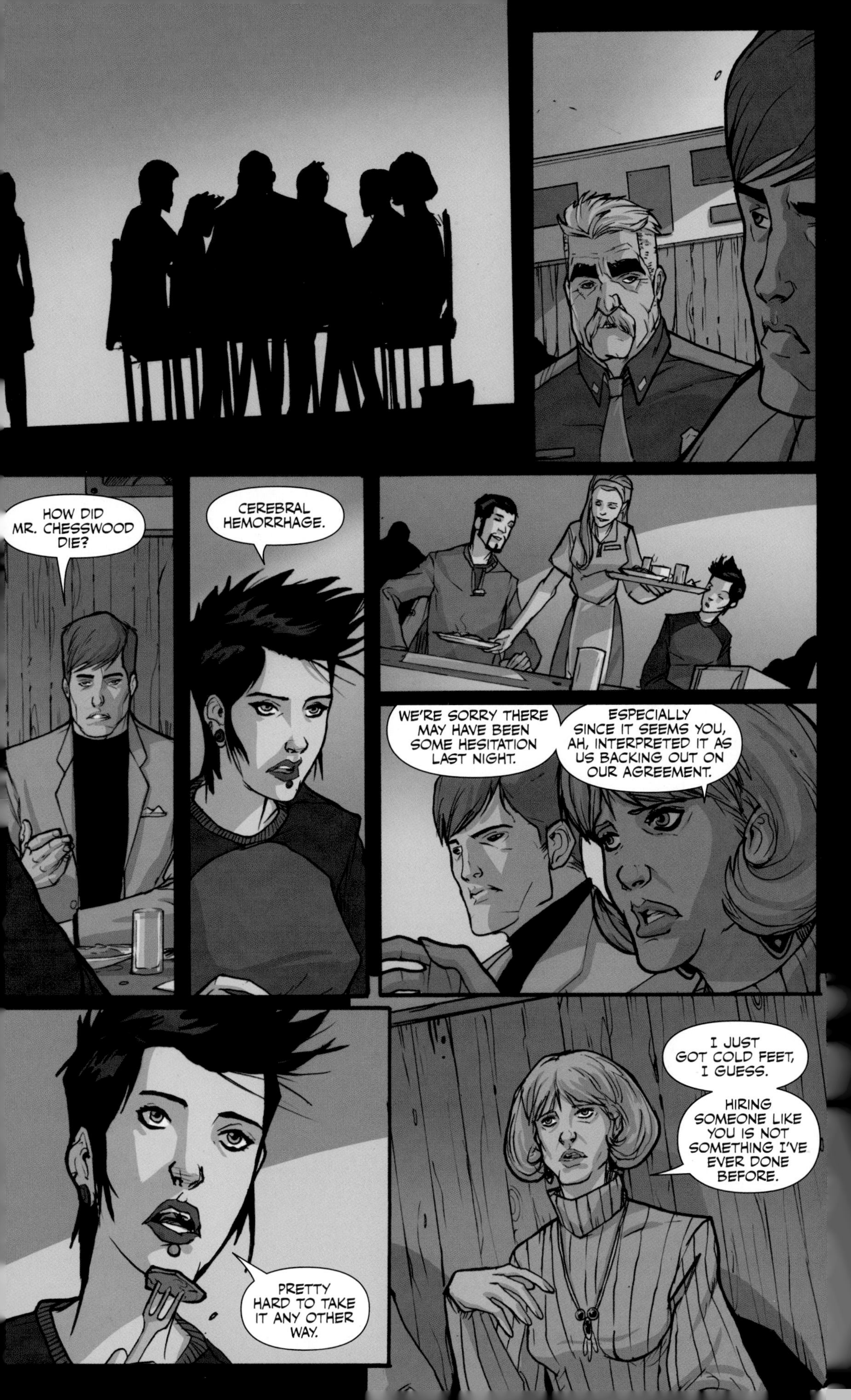
HOW DID MR. CHESSWOOD DIE?
CEREBRAL HEMORRHAGE.
WE'RE SORRY THERE MAY HAVE BEEN SOME HESITATION LAST NIGHT.
ESPECIALLY SINCE IT SEEMS YOU, AH, INTERPRETED IT AS US BACKING OUT ON OUR AGREEMENT.
PRETTY HARD TO TAKE IT ANY OTHER WAY.
I JUST GOT COLD FEET, I GUESS.
HIRING SOMEONE LIKE YOU IS NOT SOMETHING I'VE EVER DONE BEFORE.

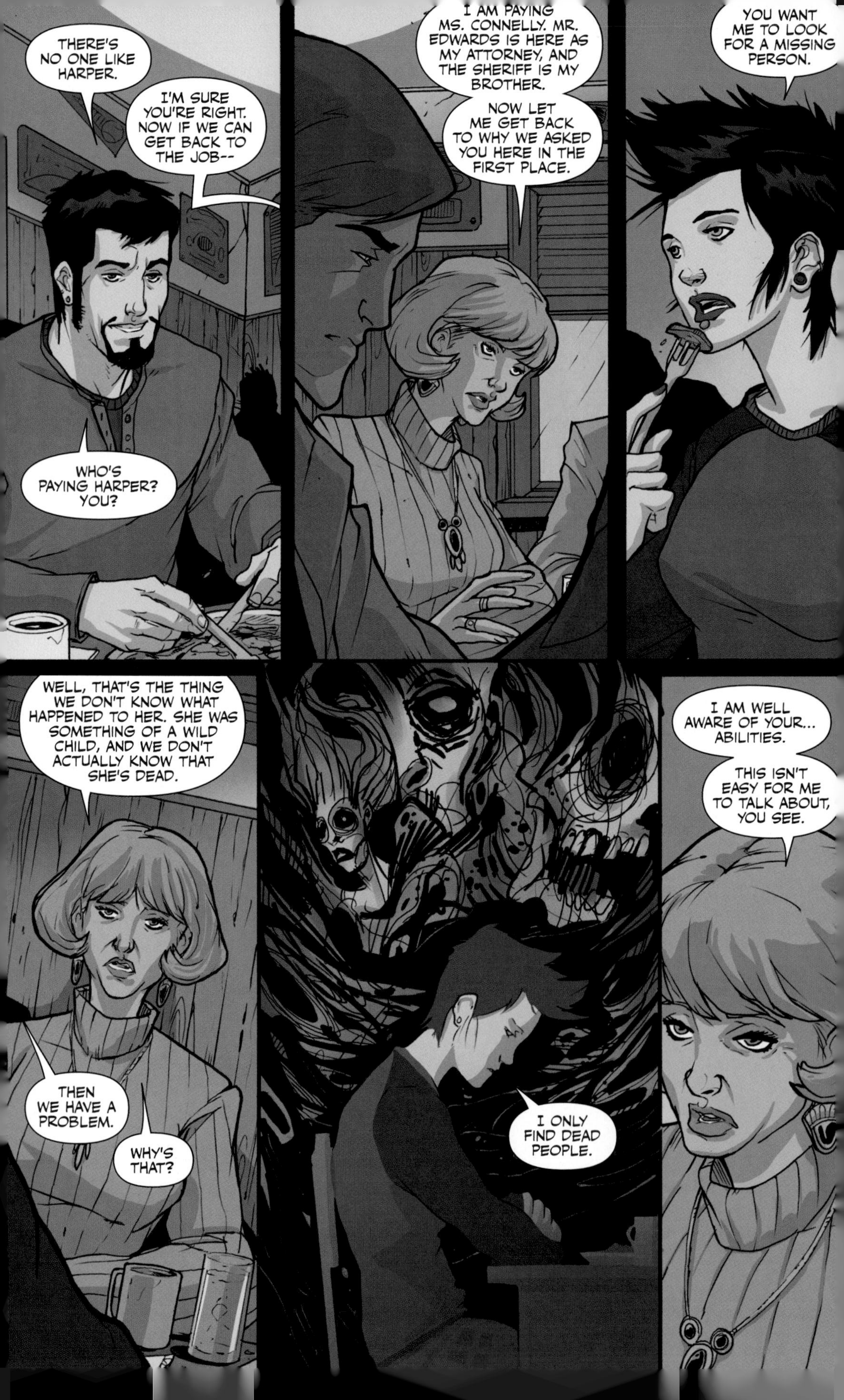
THERE'S NO ONE LIKE HARPER.
I'M SURE YOU'RE RIGHT. NOW IF WE CAN GET BACK TO THE JOB--
WHO'S PAYING HARPER? YOU?
I AM PAYING MS. CONNELLY. MR. EDWARDS IS HERE AS MY ATTORNEY, AND THE SHERIFF IS MY BROTHER.
NOW LET ME GET BACK TO WHY WE ASKED YOU HERE IN THE FIRST PLACE.
YOU WANT ME TO LOOK FOR A MISSING PERSON.
WELL, THAT'S THE THING WE DON'T KNOW WHAT HAPPENED TO HER. SHE WAS SOMETHING OF A WILD CHILD, AND WE DON'T ACTUALLY KNOW THAT SHE'S DEAD.
THEN WE HAVE A PROBLEM.
WHY'S THAT?
I ONLY FIND DEAD PEOPLE.
I AM WELL AWARE OF YOUR... ABILITIES.
THIS ISN'T EASY FOR ME TO TALK ABOUT, YOU SEE.

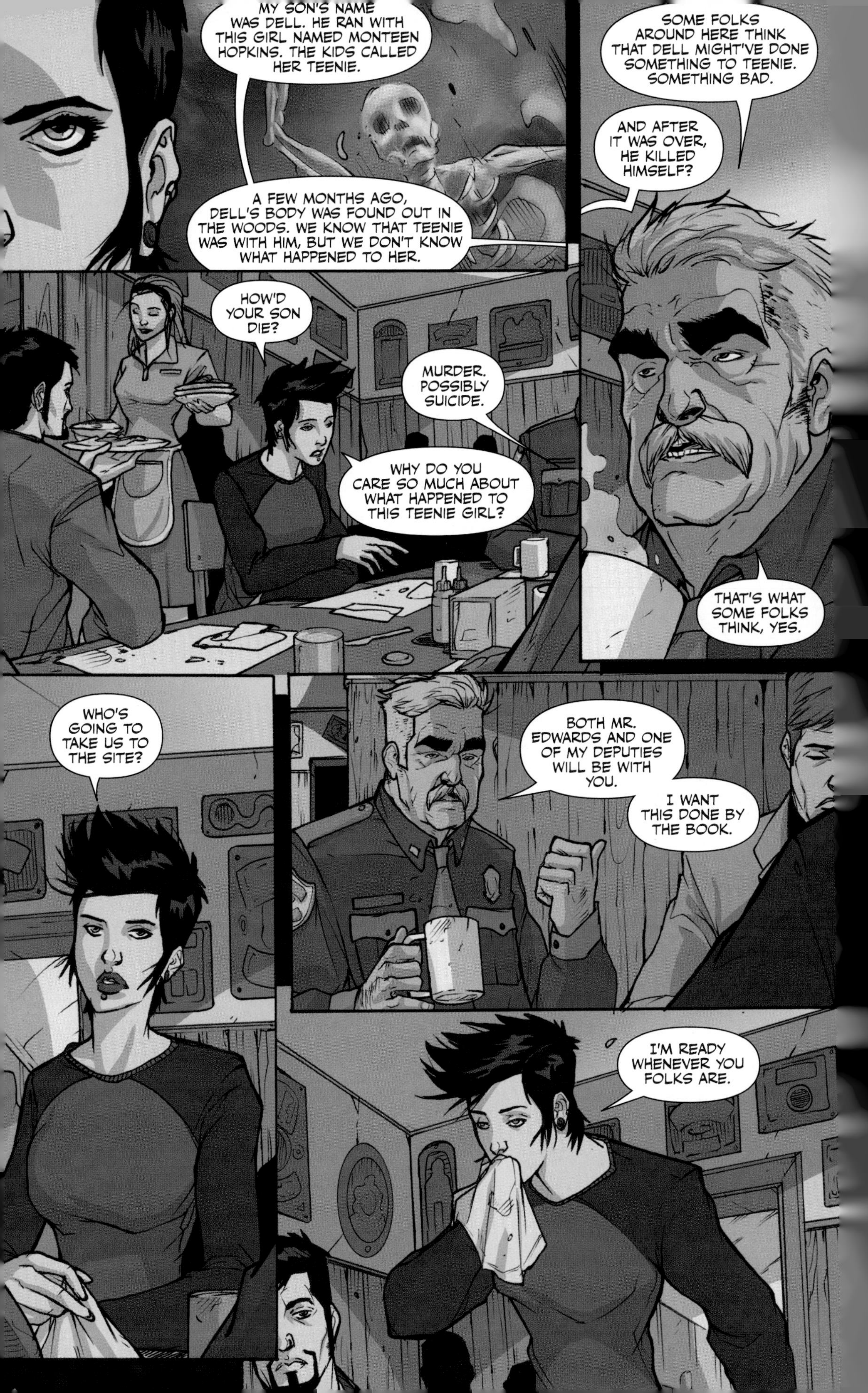
MY SON'S NAME WAS DELL. HE RAN WITH THIS GIRL NAMED MONTEEN HOPKINS. THE KIDS CALLED HER TEENIE.
A FEW MONTHS AGO, DELL'S BODY WAS FOUND OUT IN THE WOODS. WE KNOW THAT TEENIE WAS WITH HIM, BUT WE DON'T KNOW WHAT HAPPENED TO HER.
SOME FOLKS AROUND HERE THINK THAT DELL MIGHT'VE DONE SOMETHING TO TEENIE. SOMETHING BAD.
AND AFTER IT WAS OVER, HE KILLED HIMSELF?
HOW'D YOUR SON DIE?
MURDER. POSSIBLY SUICIDE.
WHY DO YOU CARE SO MUCH ABOUT WHAT HAPPENED TO THIS TEENIE GIRL?
THAT'S WHAT SOME FOLKS THINK, YES.
WHO'S GOING TO TAKE US TO THE SITE?
BOTH MR. EDWARDS AND ONE OF MY DEPUTIES WILL BE WITH YOU.
I WANT THIS DONE BY THE BOOK.
I'M READY WHENEVER YOU FOLKS ARE.

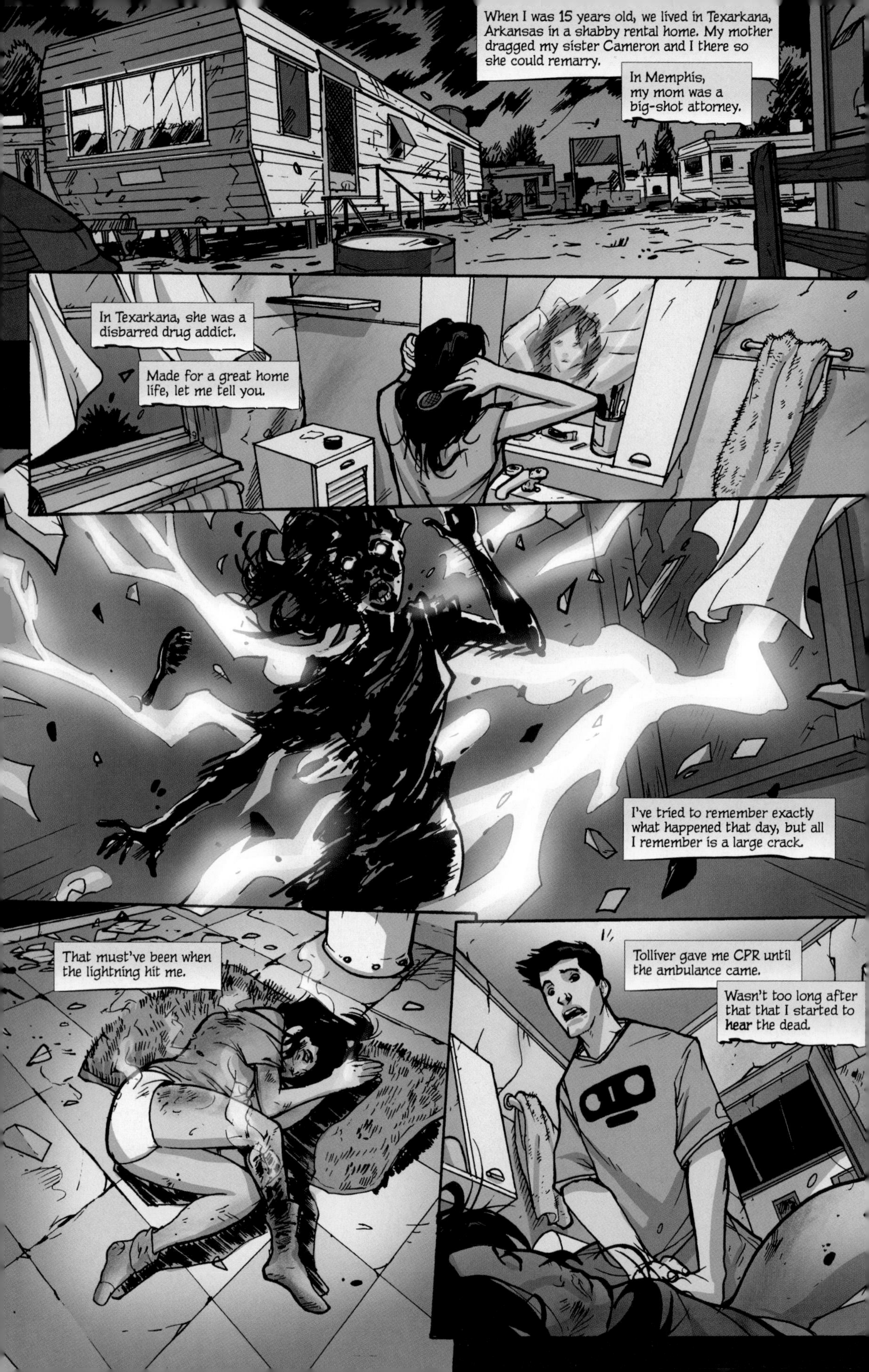
When I was 15 years old, we lived in Texarkana, Arkansas in a shabby rental home. My mother dragged my sister Cameron and I there so she could remarry.
In Memphis, my mom was a big-shot attorney.
In Texarkana, she was a disbarred drug addict.
Made for a great home life, let me tell you.
I've tried to remember exactly what happened that day, but all I remember is a large crack.
That must've been when the lightning hit me.
Tolliver gave me CPR until the ambulance came.
Wasn't too long after that that I started to **hear** the dead.

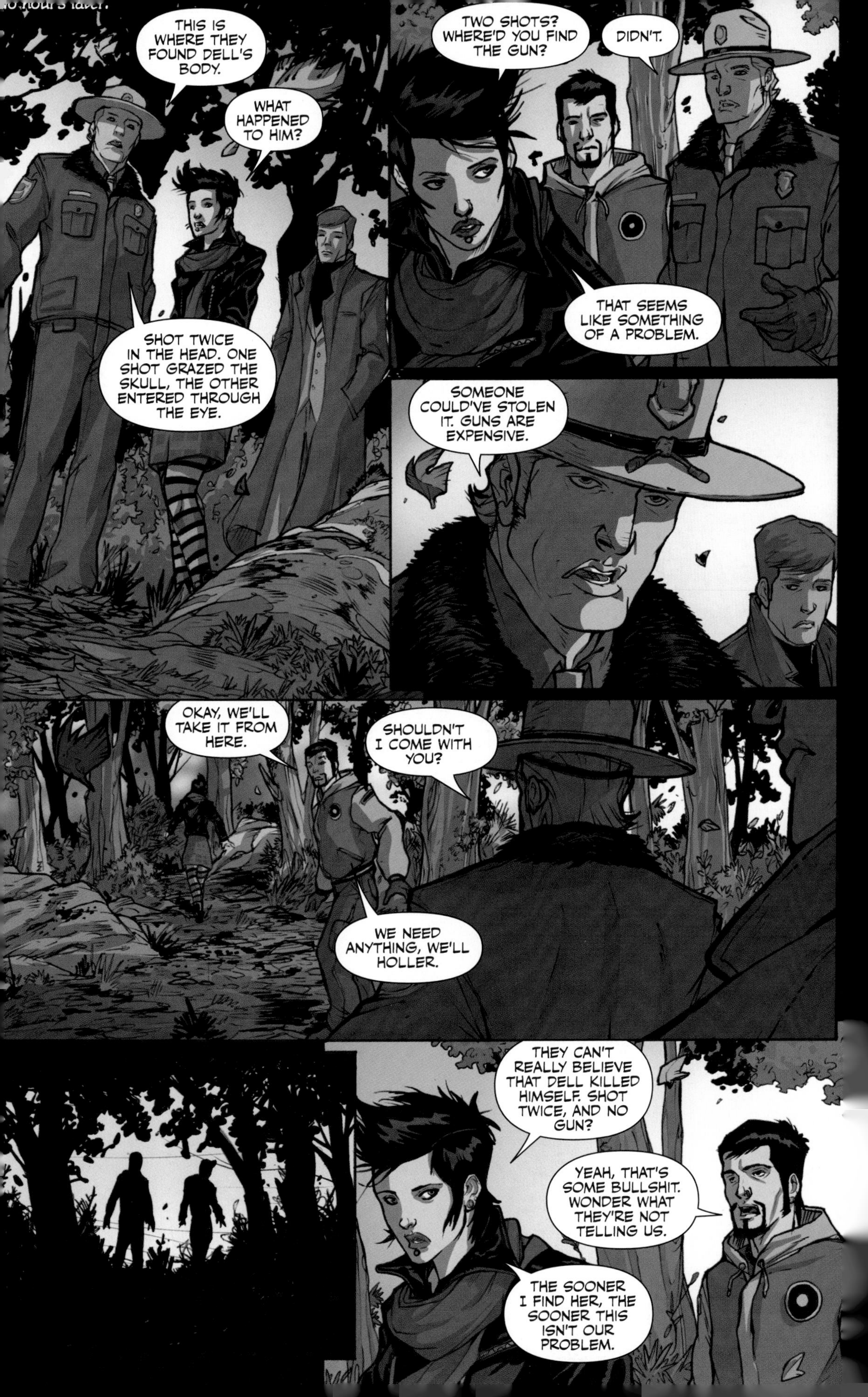
THIS IS WHERE THEY FOUND DELL'S BODY.
WHAT HAPPENED TO HIM?
SHOT TWICE IN THE HEAD. ONE SHOT GRAZED THE SKULL, THE OTHER ENTERED THROUGH THE EYE.
TWO SHOTS? WHERE'D YOU FIND THE GUN?
DIDN'T.
THAT SEEMS LIKE SOMETHING OF A PROBLEM.
SOMEONE COULD'VE STOLEN IT. GUNS ARE EXPENSIVE.
OKAY, WE'LL TAKE IT FROM HERE.
SHOULDN'T I COME WITH YOU?
WE NEED ANYTHING, WE'LL HOLLER.
THEY CAN'T REALLY BELIEVE THAT DELL KILLED HIMSELF. SHOT TWICE, AND NO GUN?
YEAH, THAT'S SOME BULLSHIT. WONDER WHAT THEY'RE NOT TELLING US.
THE SOONER I FIND HER, THE SOONER THIS ISN'T OUR PROBLEM.

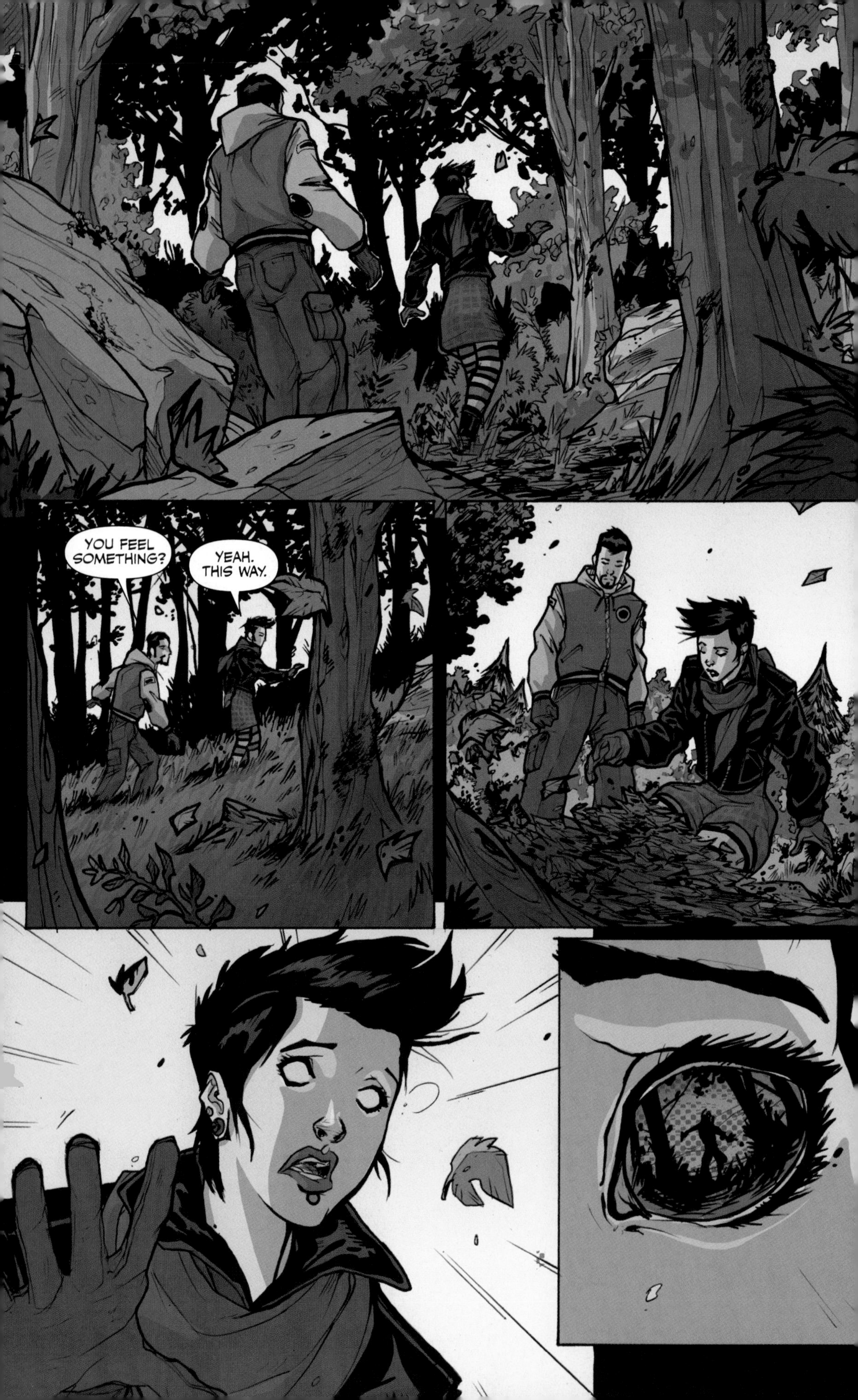
YOU FEEL SOMETHING?
YEAH. THIS WAY.

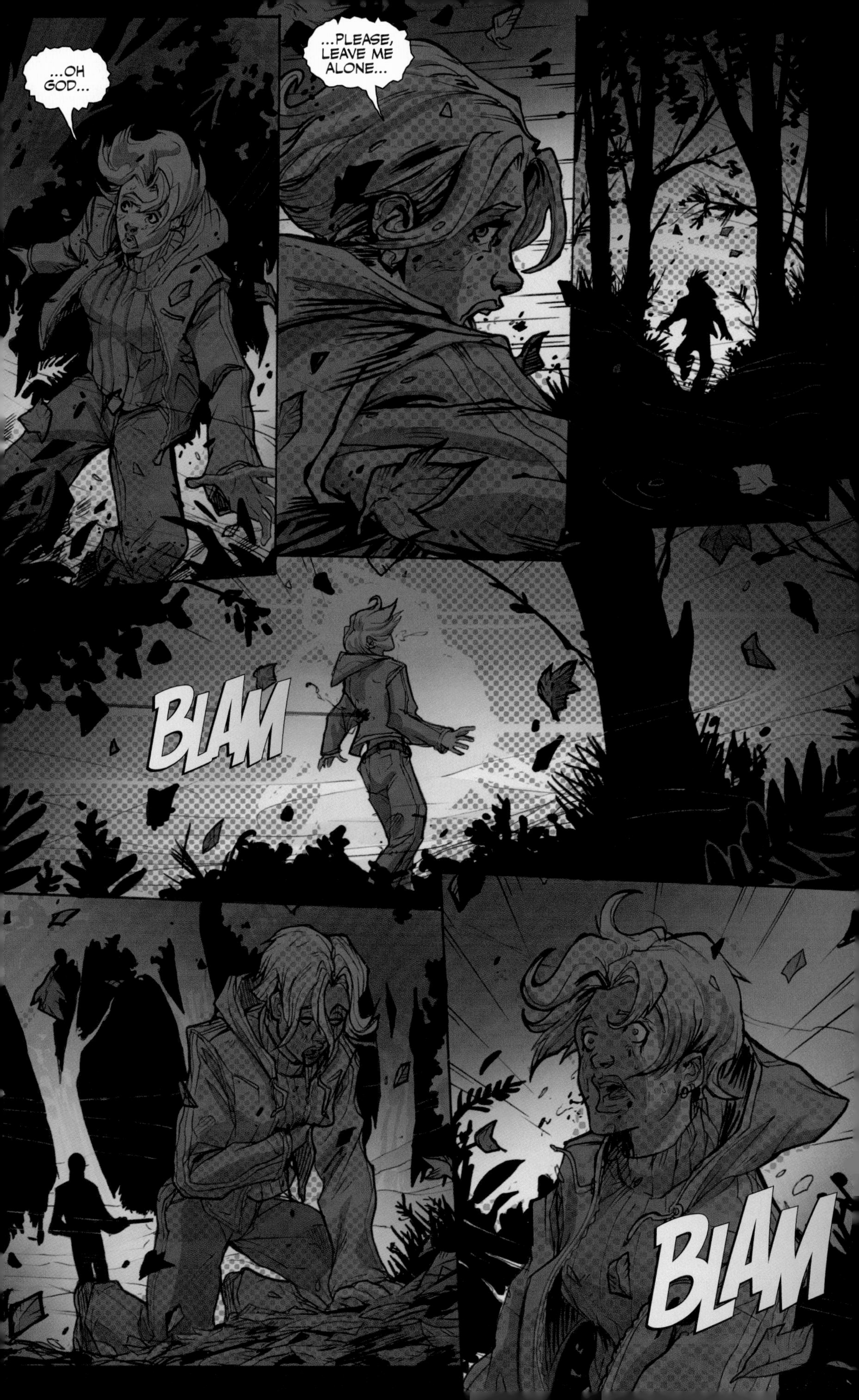
...OH GOD...
...PLEASE, LEAVE ME ALONE...
BLAM
BLAM

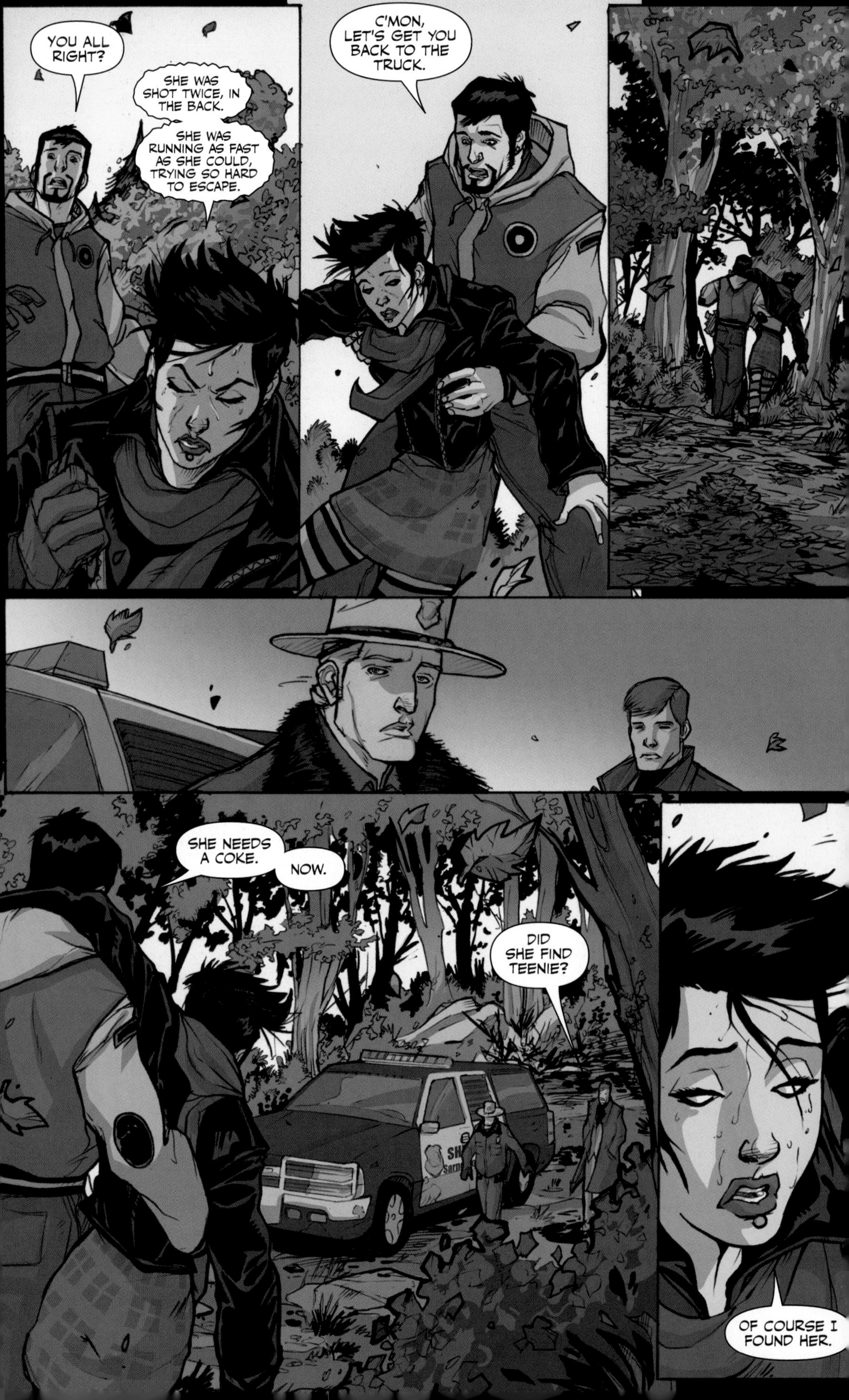
YOU ALL RIGHT?
SHE WAS SHOT TWICE, IN THE BACK.
SHE WAS RUNNING AS FAST AS SHE COULD, TRYING SO HARD TO ESCAPE.
C'MON, LET'S GET YOU BACK TO THE TRUCK.
SHE NEEDS A COKE.
NOW.
DID SHE FIND TEENIE?
OF COURSE I FOUND HER.

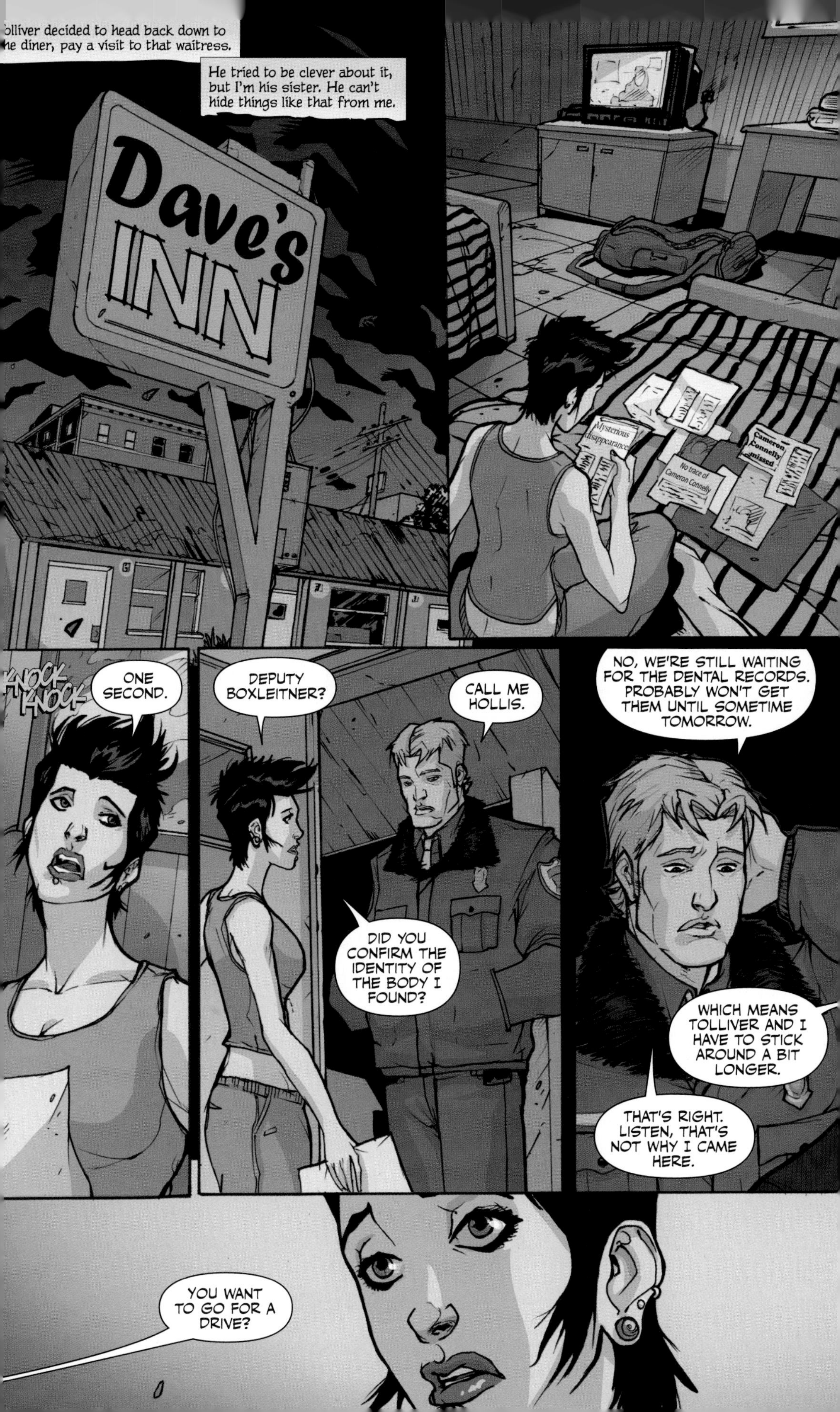
olliver decided to head back down to he diner, pay a visit to that waitress.
He tried to be clever about it, but I'm his sister. He can't hide things like that from me.
Dave's INN
Mysterious disappearance
Cameron Connelly missed
No trace of Cameron Connelly
KNOCK KNOCK
ONE SECOND.
DEPUTY BOXLEITNER?
CALL ME HOLLIS.
DID YOU CONFIRM THE IDENTITY OF THE BODY I FOUND?
NO, WE'RE STILL WAITING FOR THE DENTAL RECORDS. PROBABLY WON'T GET THEM UNTIL SOMETIME TOMORROW.
WHICH MEANS TOLLIVER AND I HAVE TO STICK AROUND A BIT LONGER.
THAT'S RIGHT. LISTEN, THAT'S NOT WHY I CAME HERE.
YOU WANT TO GO FOR A DRIVE?

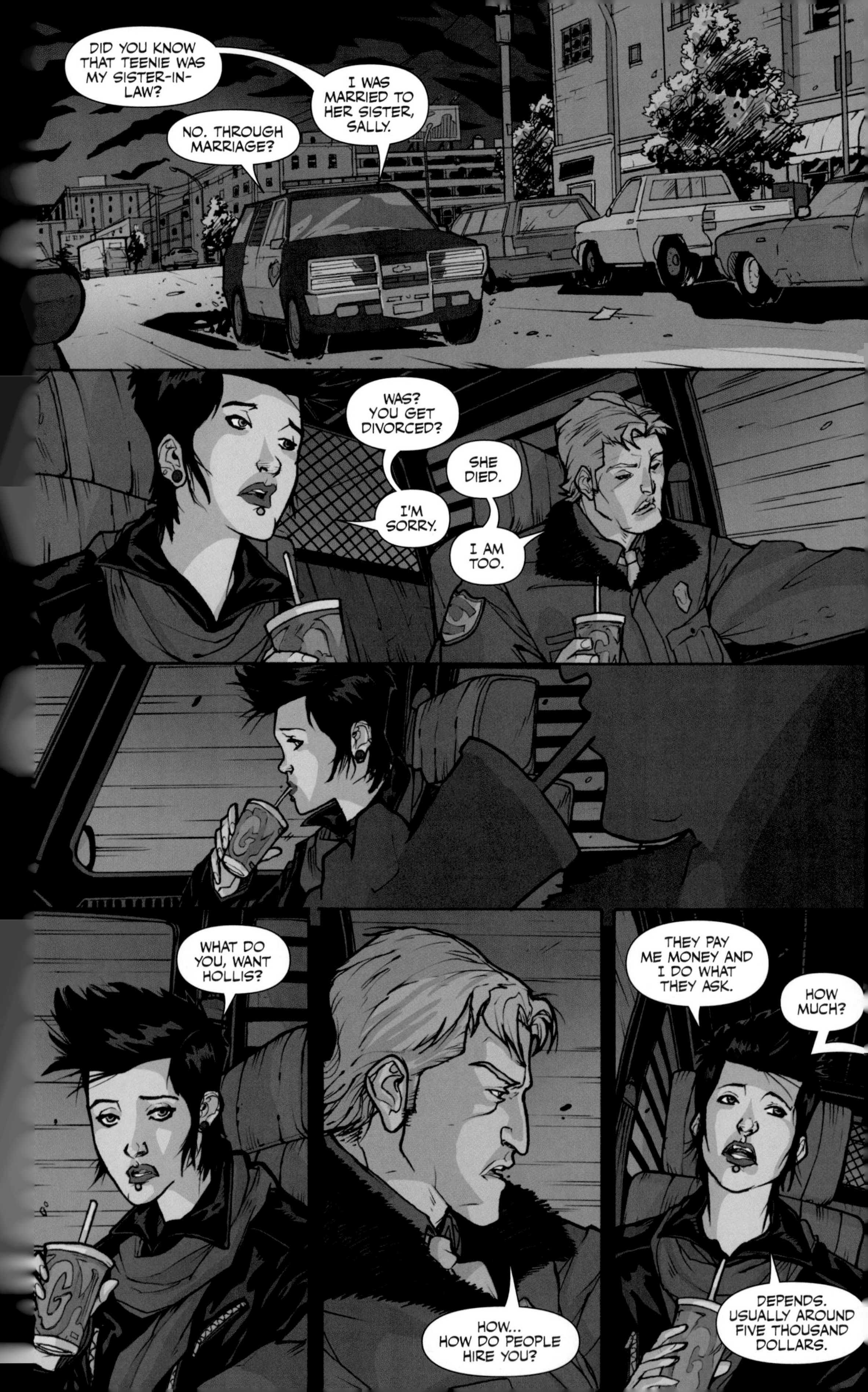
DID YOU KNOW THAT TEENIE WAS MY SISTER-IN-LAW?
NO. THROUGH MARRIAGE?
I WAS MARRIED TO HER SISTER, SALLY.
WAS? YOU GET DIVORCED?
SHE DIED.
I'M SORRY.
I AM TOO.
WHAT DO YOU, WANT HOLLIS?
HOW... HOW DO PEOPLE HIRE YOU?
THEY PAY ME MONEY AND I DO WHAT THEY ASK.
HOW MUCH?
DEPENDS. USUALLY AROUND FIVE THOUSAND DOLLARS.

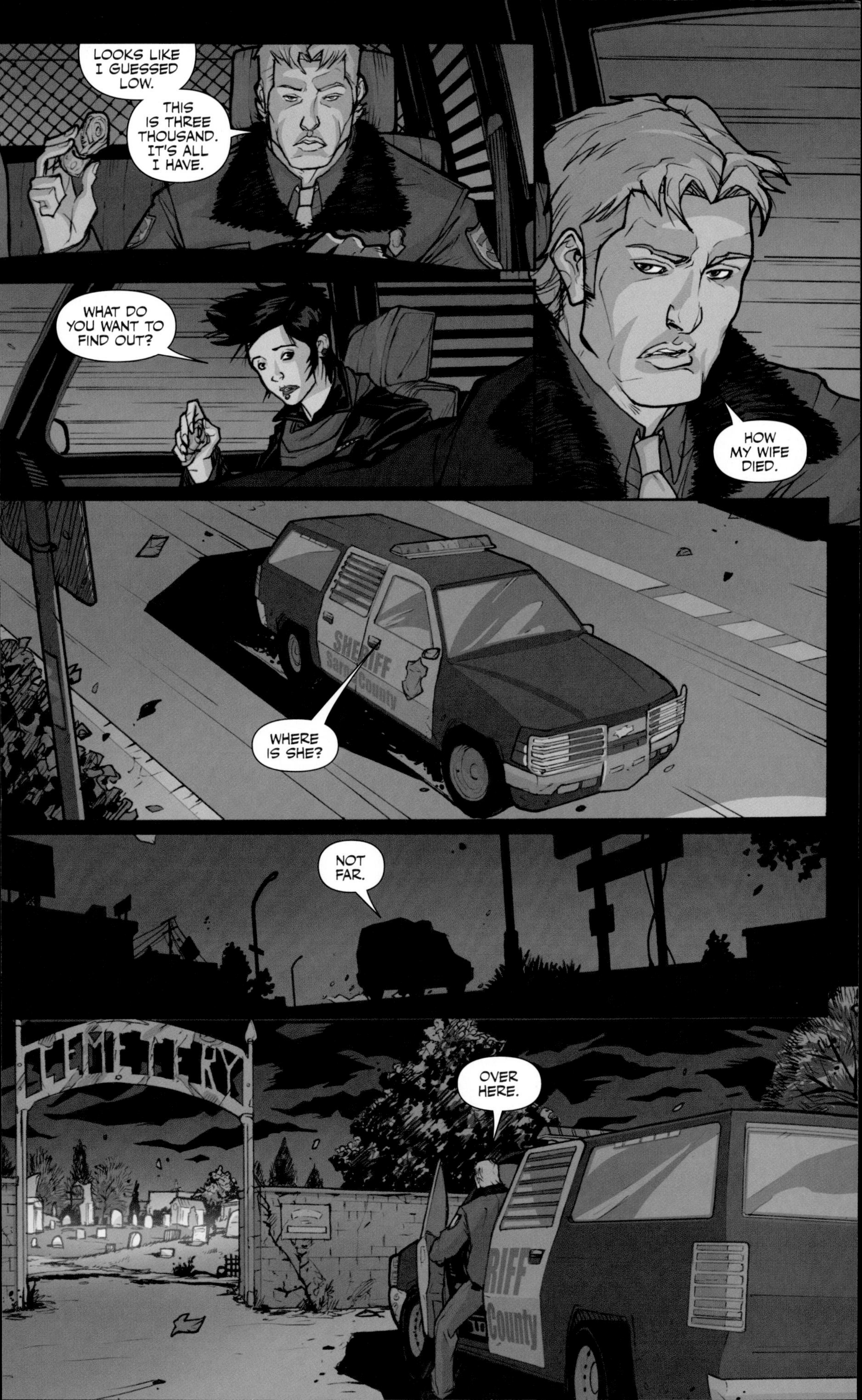
LOOKS LIKE I GUESSED LOW.
THIS IS THREE THOUSAND. IT'S ALL I HAVE.
WHAT DO YOU WANT TO FIND OUT?
HOW MY WIFE DIED.
SHERIFF
WHERE IS SHE?
NOT FAR.
CEMETERY
OVER HERE.
RIFF
County

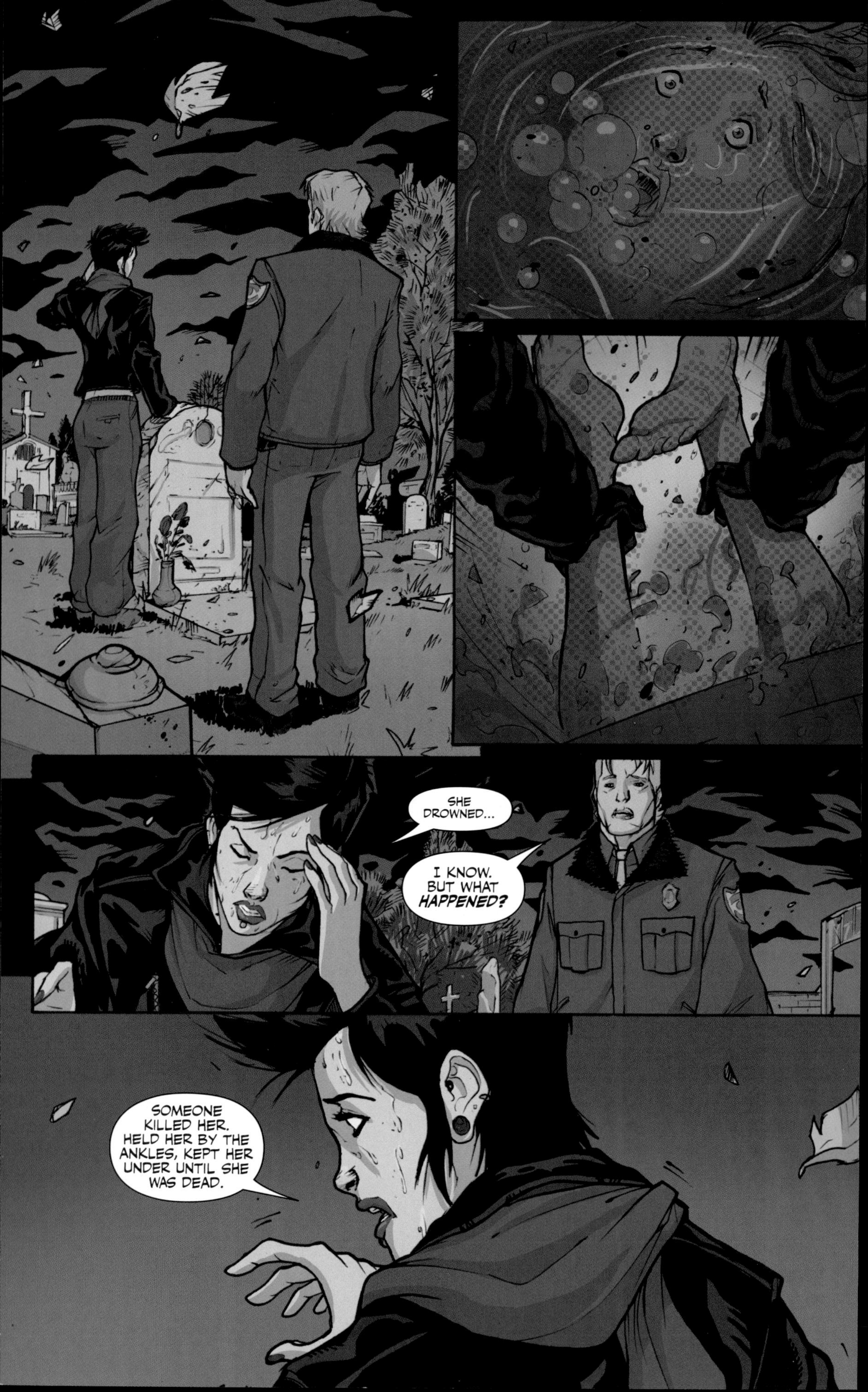
SHE DROWNED...
I KNOW. BUT WHAT *HAPPENED?*
SOMEONE KILLED HER. HELD HER BY THE ANKLES, KEPT HER UNDER UNTIL SHE WAS DEAD.

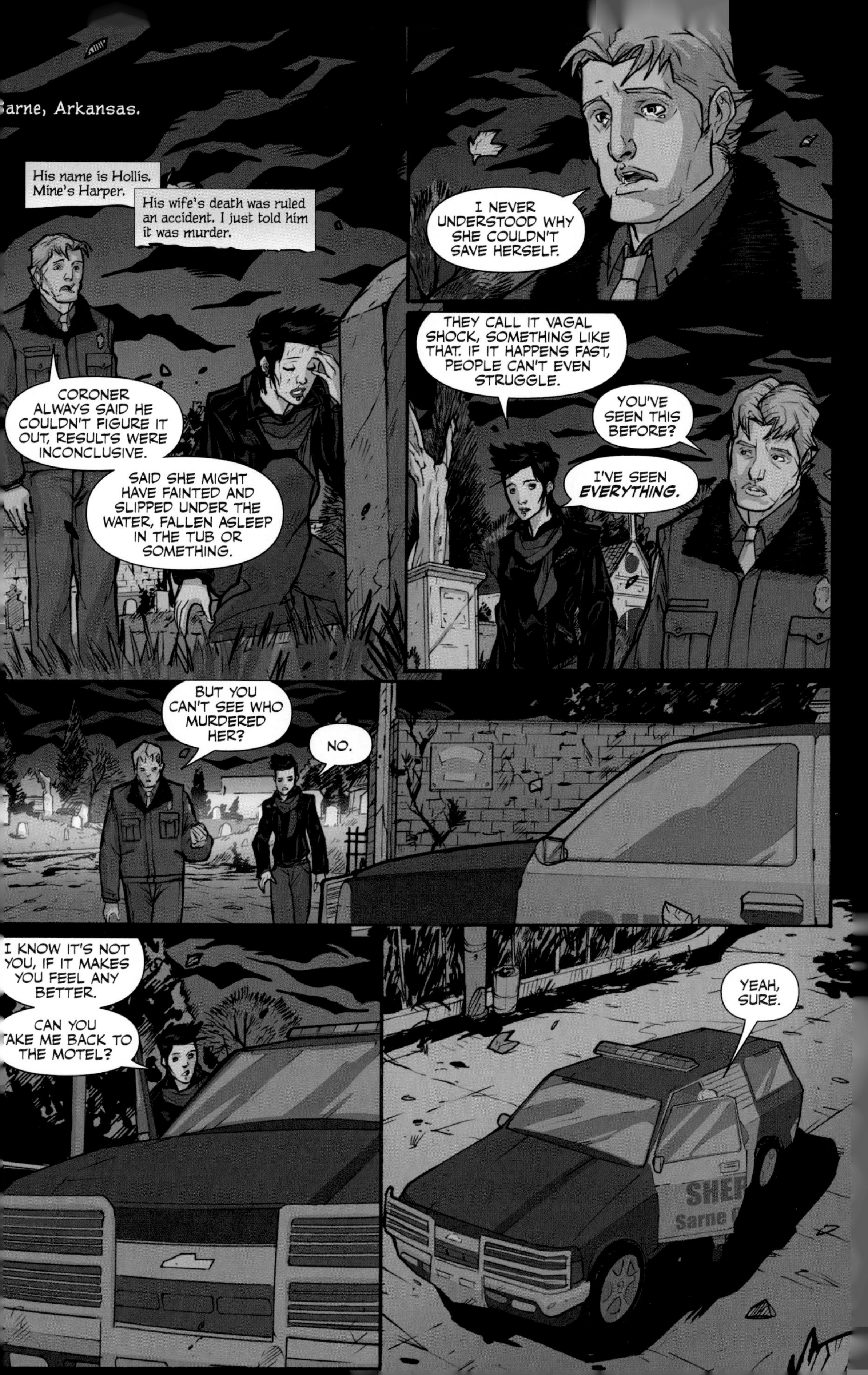
arne, Arkansas.
His name is Hollis. Mine's Harper.
His wife's death was ruled an accident. I just told him it was murder.
CORONER ALWAYS SAID HE COULDN'T FIGURE IT OUT, RESULTS WERE INCONCLUSIVE.
SAID SHE MIGHT HAVE FAINTED AND SLIPPED UNDER THE WATER, FALLEN ASLEEP IN THE TUB OR SOMETHING.
I NEVER UNDERSTOOD WHY SHE COULDN'T SAVE HERSELF.
THEY CALL IT VAGAL SHOCK, SOMETHING LIKE THAT. IF IT HAPPENS FAST, PEOPLE CAN'T EVEN STRUGGLE.
YOU'VE SEEN THIS BEFORE?
I'VE SEEN *EVERYTHING.*
BUT YOU CAN'T SEE WHO MURDERED HER?
NO.
I KNOW IT'S NOT YOU, IF IT MAKES YOU FEEL ANY BETTER.
CAN YOU AKE ME BACK TO THE MOTEL?
YEAH, SURE.

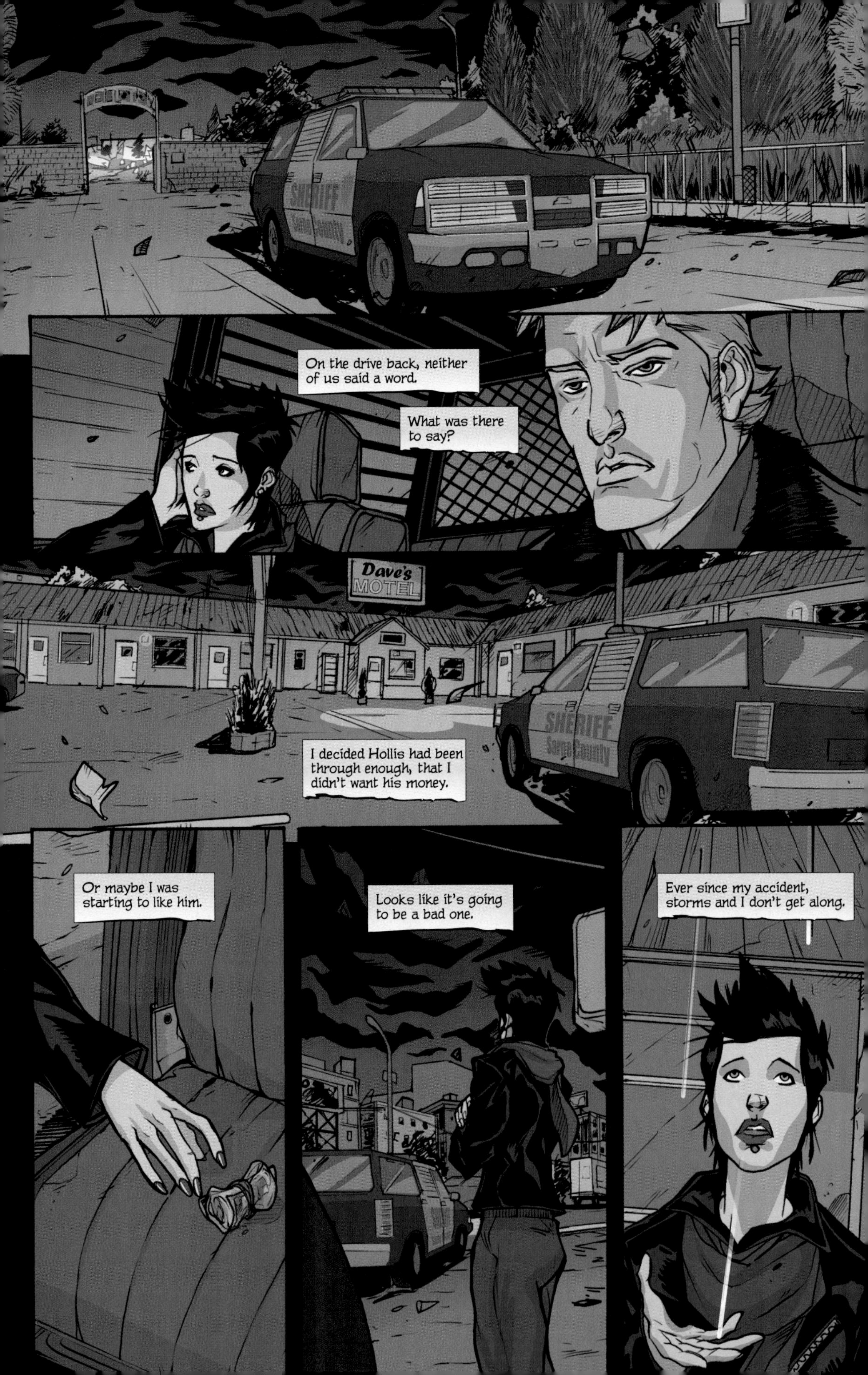
SHERIFF
Sarge County
On the drive back, neither of us said a word.
What was there to say?
Dave's
MOTEL
SHERIFF
Sarge County
I decided Hollis had been through enough, that I didn't want his money.
Or maybe I was starting to like him.
Looks like it's going to be a bad one.
Ever since my accident, storms and I don't get along.

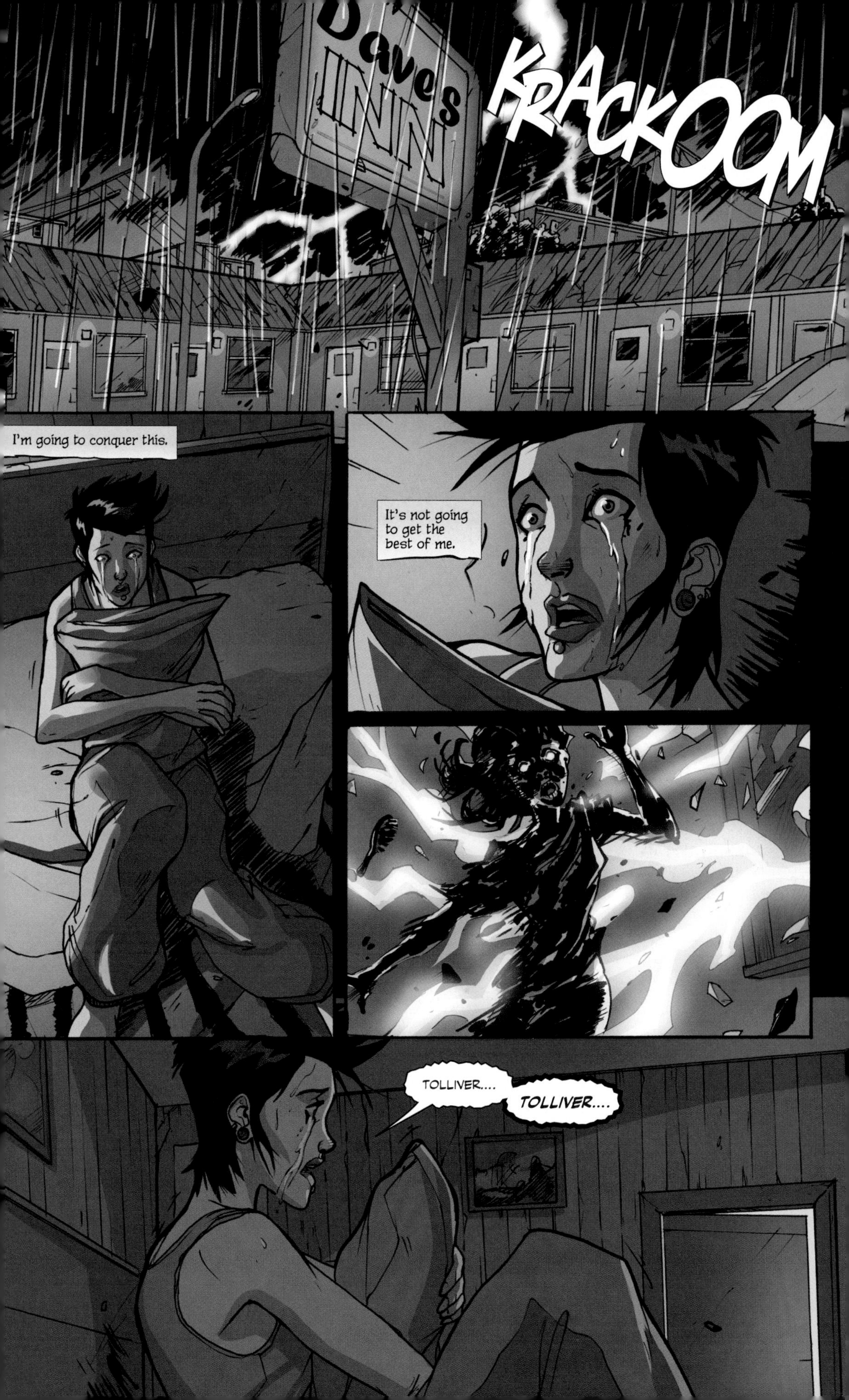
Dave's INN
KRACKOOM
I'm going to conquer this.
It's not going to get the best of me.
TOLLIVER....
TOLLIVER....

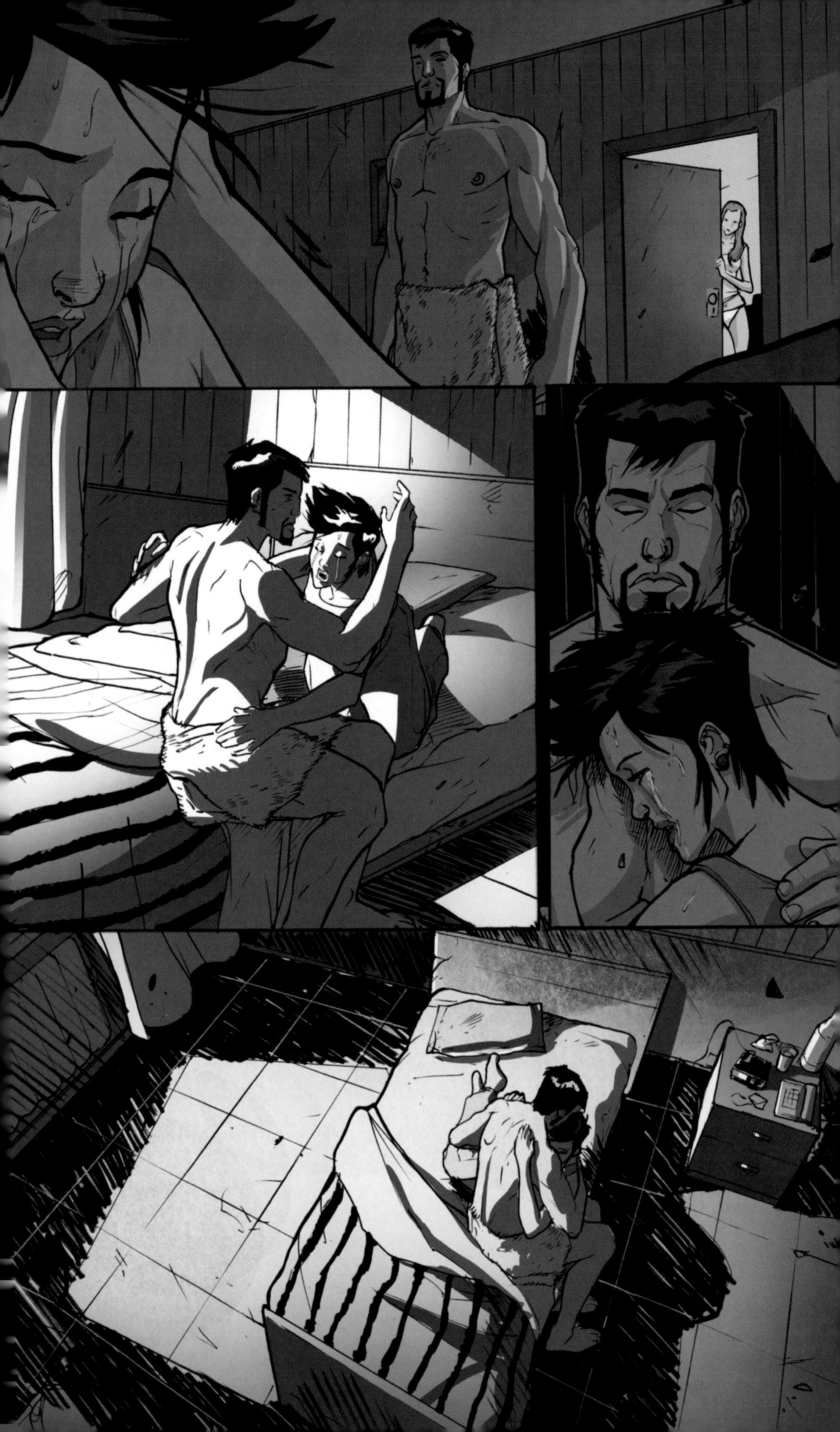

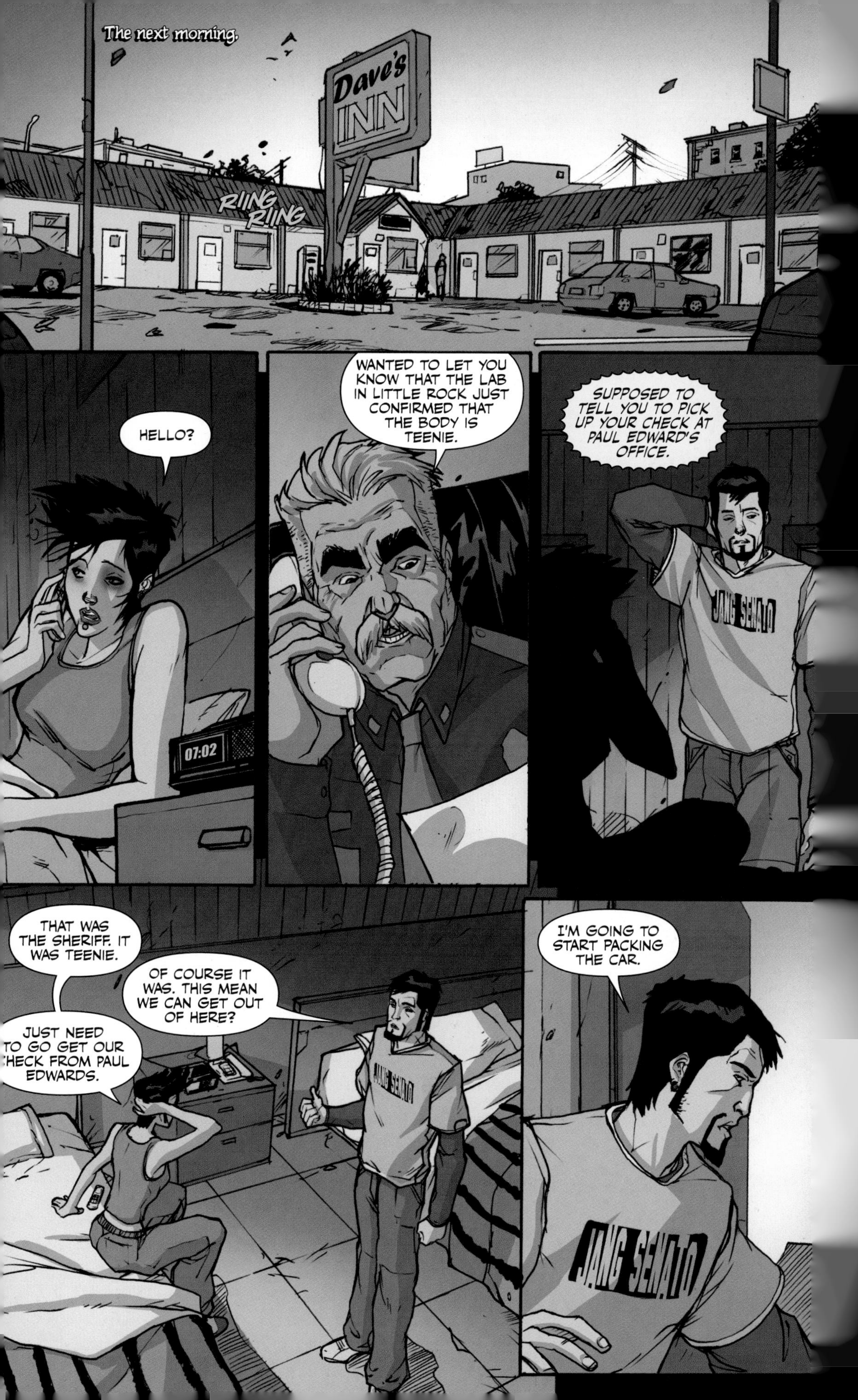
The next morning.
Dave's INN
RIING RIING
HELLO?
07:02
WANTED TO LET YOU KNOW THAT THE LAB IN LITTLE ROCK JUST CONFIRMED THAT THE BODY IS TEENIE.
SUPPOSED TO TELL YOU TO PICK UP YOUR CHECK AT PAUL EDWARD'S OFFICE.
JANG SENATO
THAT WAS THE SHERIFF. IT WAS TEENIE.
OF COURSE IT WAS. THIS MEAN WE CAN GET OUT OF HERE?
JUST NEED TO GO GET OUR HECK FROM PAUL EDWARDS.
I'M GOING TO START PACKING THE CAR.

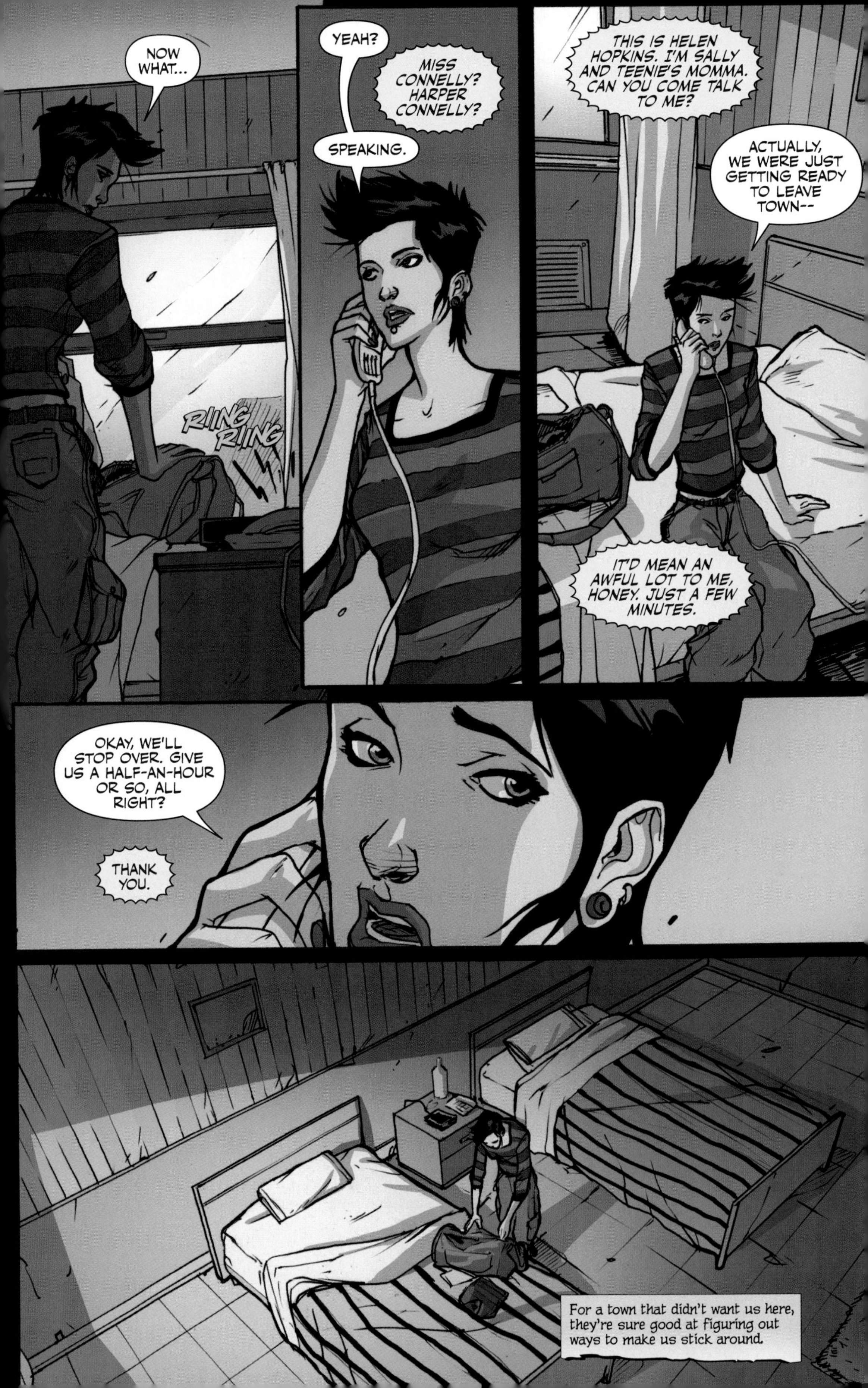
NOW WHAT...
RIING RIING
YEAH?
MISS CONNELLY? HARPER CONNELLY?
SPEAKING.
THIS IS HELEN HOPKINS. I'M SALLY AND TEENIE'S MOMMA. CAN YOU COME TALK TO ME?
ACTUALLY, WE WERE JUST GETTING READY TO LEAVE TOWN--
IT'D MEAN AN AWFUL LOT TO ME, HONEY. JUST A FEW MINUTES.
OKAY, WE'LL STOP OVER. GIVE US A HALF-AN-HOUR OR SO, ALL RIGHT?
THANK YOU.
For a town that didn't want us here, they're sure good at figuring out ways to make us stick around.

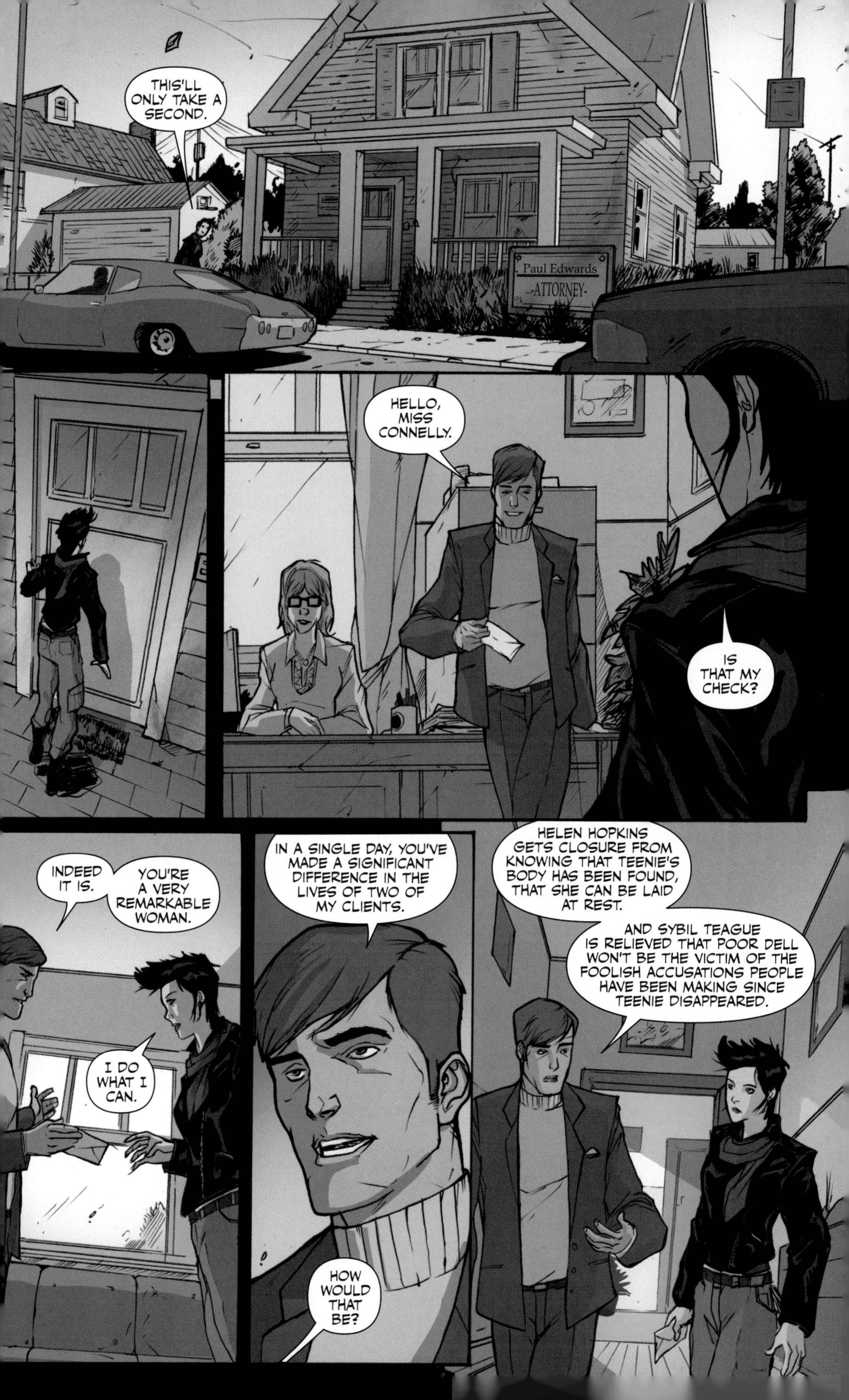
THIS'LL ONLY TAKE A SECOND.
Paul Edwards
-ATTORNEY-
HELLO, MISS CONNELLY.
IS THAT MY CHECK?
INDEED IT IS.
YOU'RE A VERY REMARKABLE WOMAN.
I DO WHAT I CAN.
IN A SINGLE DAY, YOU'VE MADE A SIGNIFICANT DIFFERENCE IN THE LIVES OF TWO OF MY CLIENTS.
HOW WOULD THAT BE?
HELEN HOPKINS GETS CLOSURE FROM KNOWING THAT TEENIE'S BODY HAS BEEN FOUND, THAT SHE CAN BE LAID AT REST.
AND SYBIL TEAGUE IS RELIEVED THAT POOR DELL WON'T BE THE VICTIM OF THE FOOLISH ACCUSATIONS PEOPLE HAVE BEEN MAKING SINCE TEENIE DISAPPEARED.

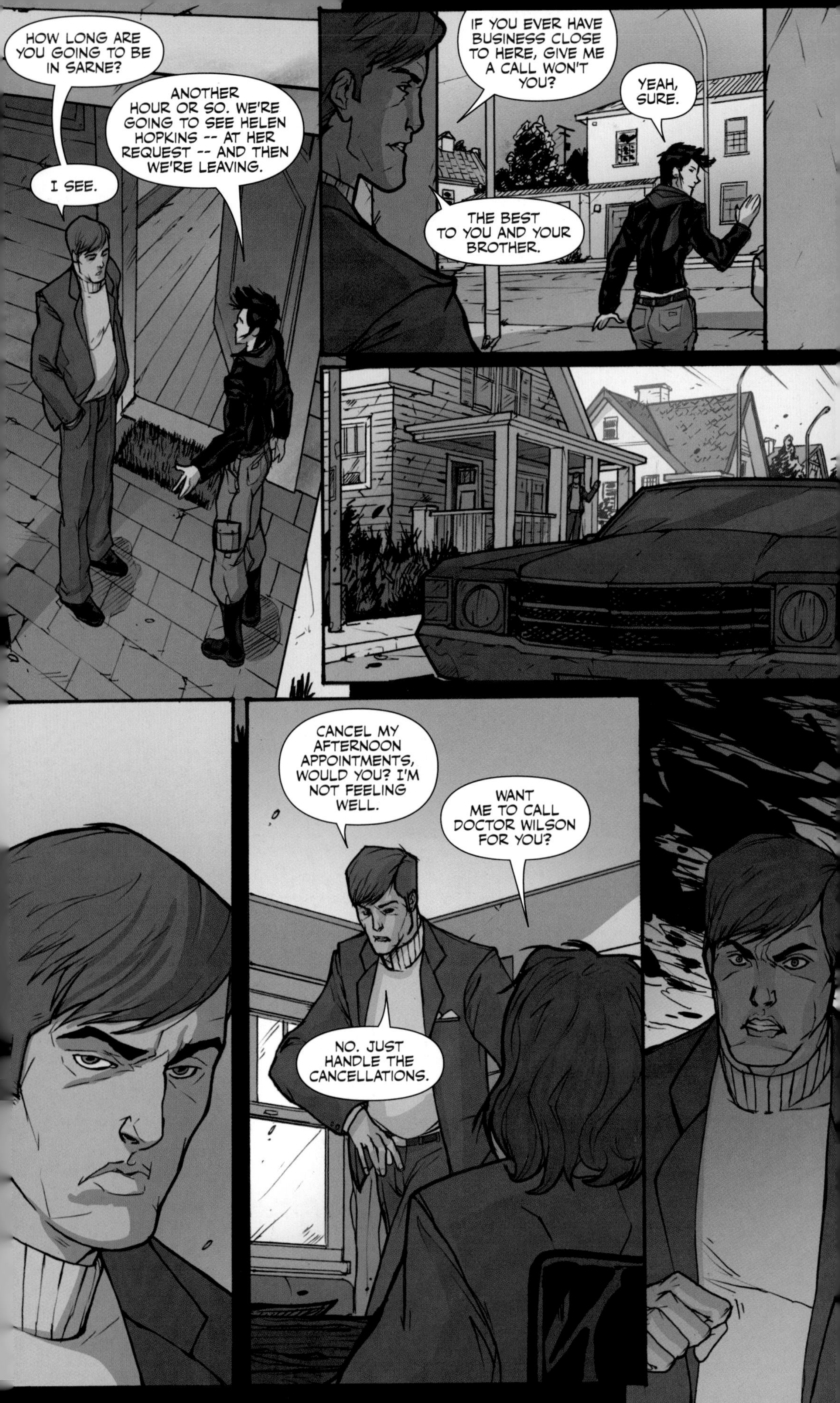
HOW LONG ARE YOU GOING TO BE IN SARNE?
ANOTHER HOUR OR SO. WE'RE GOING TO SEE HELEN HOPKINS -- AT HER REQUEST -- AND THEN WE'RE LEAVING.
I SEE.
IF YOU EVER HAVE BUSINESS CLOSE TO HERE, GIVE ME A CALL WON'T YOU?
YEAH, SURE.
THE BEST TO YOU AND YOUR BROTHER.
CANCEL MY AFTERNOON APPOINTMENTS, WOULD YOU? I'M NOT FEELING WELL.
WANT ME TO CALL DOCTOR WILSON FOR YOU?
NO. JUST HANDLE THE CANCELLATIONS.

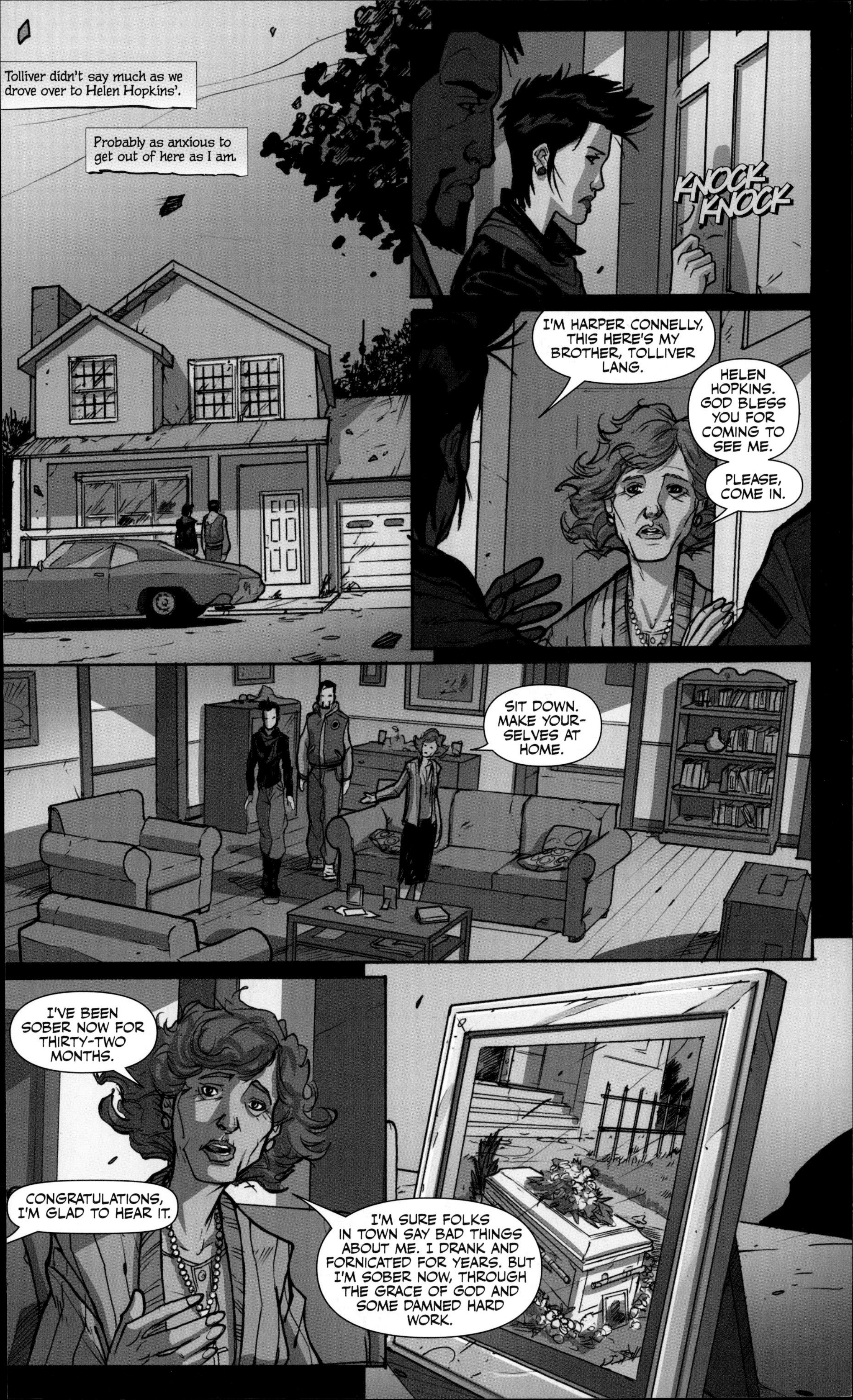
Tolliver didn't say much as we drove over to Helen Hopkins'.
Probably as anxious to get out of here as I am.
KNOCK KNOCK
I'M HARPER CONNELLY, THIS HERE'S MY BROTHER, TOLLIVER LANG.
HELEN HOPKINS. GOD BLESS YOU FOR COMING TO SEE ME.
PLEASE, COME IN.
SIT DOWN. MAKE YOUR-SELVES AT HOME.
I'VE BEEN SOBER NOW FOR THIRTY-TWO MONTHS.
CONGRATULATIONS, I'M GLAD TO HEAR IT.
I'M SURE FOLKS IN TOWN SAY BAD THINGS ABOUT ME. I DRANK AND FORNICATED FOR YEARS. BUT I'M SOBER NOW, THROUGH THE GRACE OF GOD AND SOME DAMNED HARD WORK.

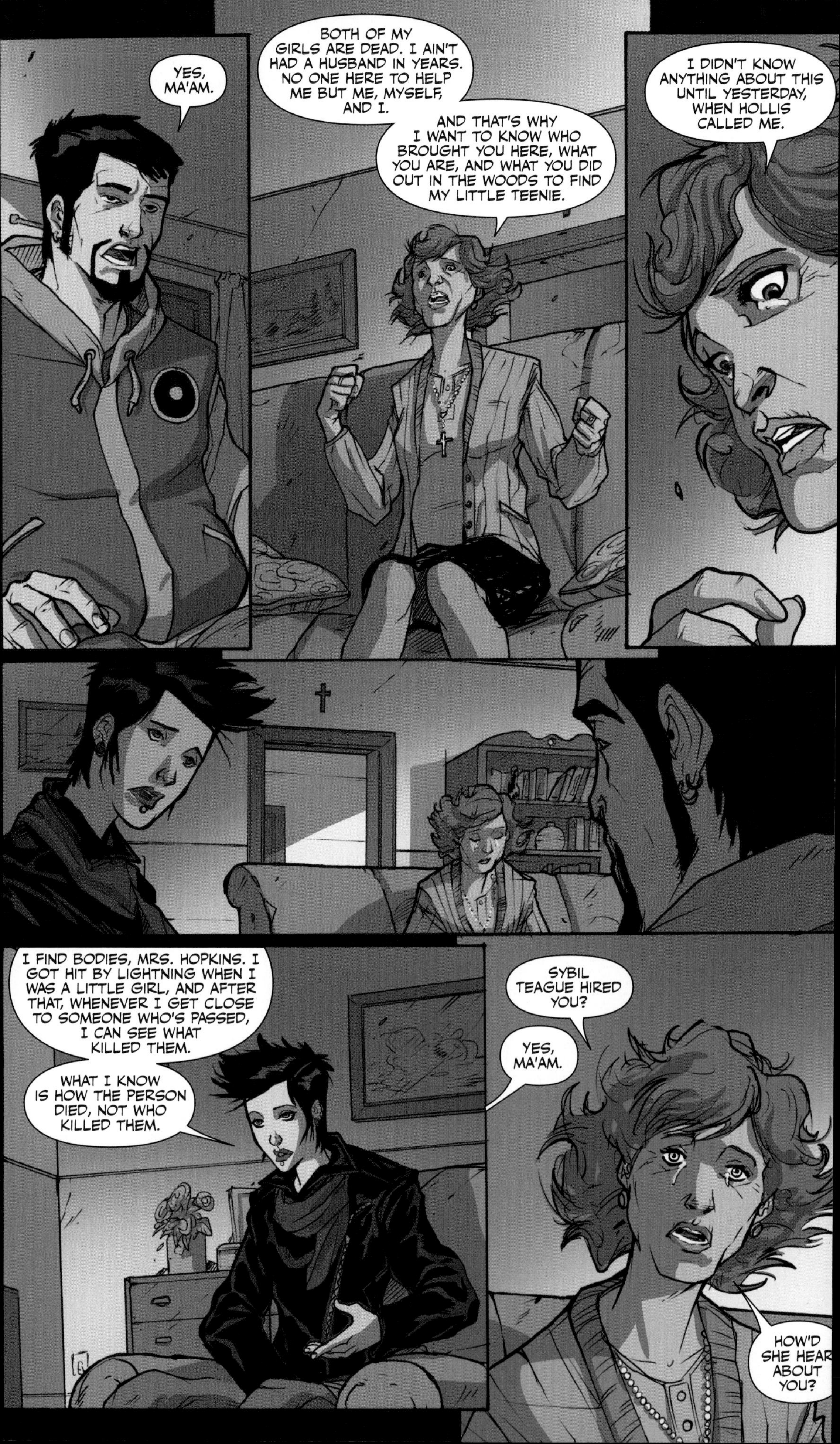
YES, MA'AM.
BOTH OF MY GIRLS ARE DEAD. I AIN'T HAD A HUSBAND IN YEARS. NO ONE HERE TO HELP ME BUT ME, MYSELF, AND I.
AND THAT'S WHY I WANT TO KNOW WHO BROUGHT YOU HERE, WHAT YOU ARE, AND WHAT YOU DID OUT IN THE WOODS TO FIND MY LITTLE TEENIE.
I DIDN'T KNOW ANYTHING ABOUT THIS UNTIL YESTERDAY, WHEN HOLLIS CALLED ME.
I FIND BODIES, MRS. HOPKINS. I GOT HIT BY LIGHTNING WHEN I WAS A LITTLE GIRL, AND AFTER THAT, WHENEVER I GET CLOSE TO SOMEONE WHO'S PASSED, I CAN SEE WHAT KILLED THEM.
WHAT I KNOW IS HOW THE PERSON DIED, NOT WHO KILLED THEM.
SYBIL TEAGUE HIRED YOU?
YES, MA'AM.
HOW'D SHE HEAR ABOUT YOU?

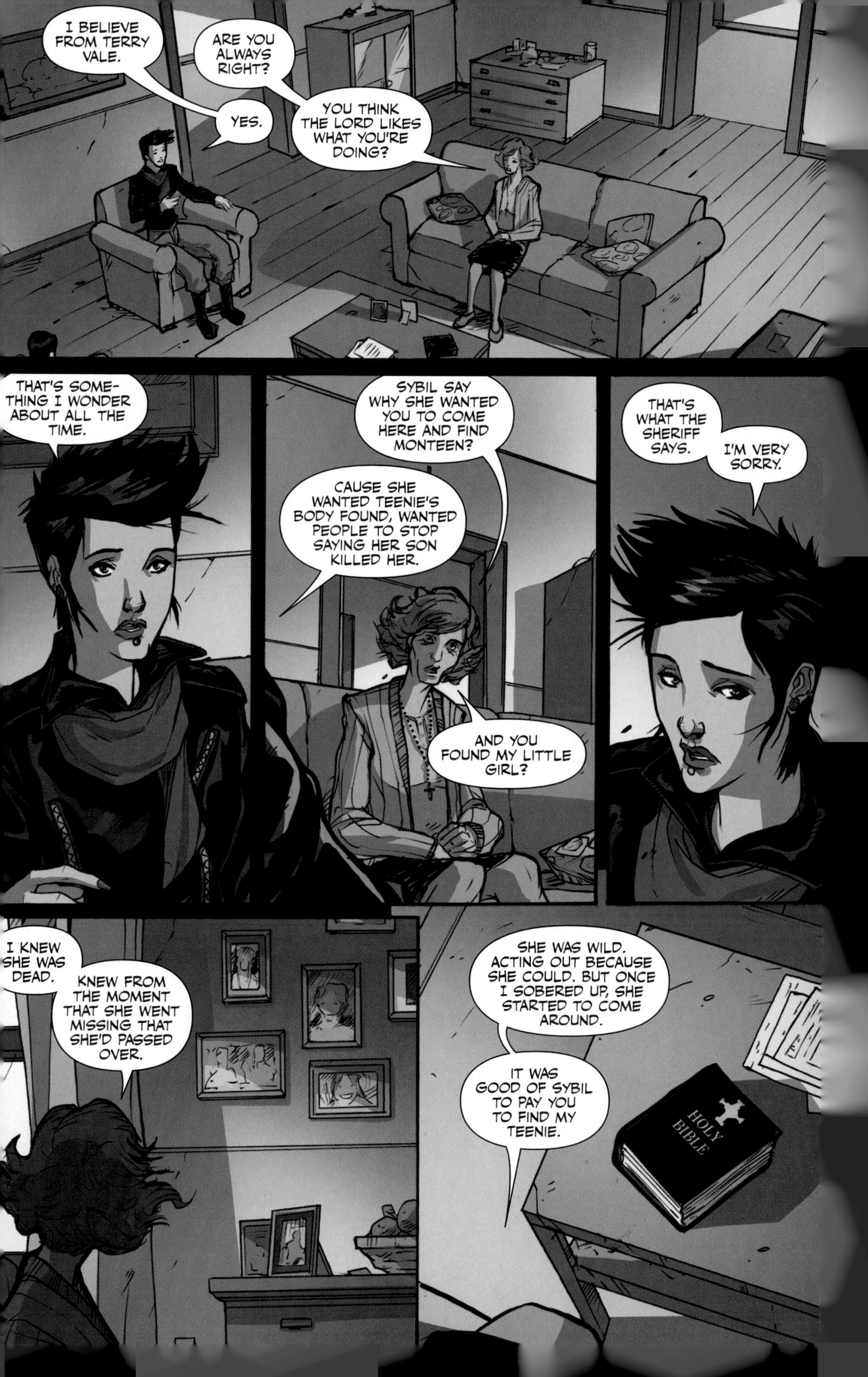

I BELIEVE FROM TERRY VALE.
ARE YOU ALWAYS RIGHT?
YES.
YOU THINK THE LORD LIKES WHAT YOU'RE DOING?
THAT'S SOME-THING I WONDER ABOUT ALL THE TIME.
SYBIL SAY WHY SHE WANTED YOU TO COME HERE AND FIND MONTEEN?
CAUSE SHE WANTED TEENIE'S BODY FOUND, WANTED PEOPLE TO STOP SAYING HER SON KILLED HER.
AND YOU FOUND MY LITTLE GIRL?
THAT'S WHAT THE SHERIFF SAYS.
I'M VERY SORRY.
I KNEW SHE WAS DEAD.
KNEW FROM THE MOMENT THAT SHE WENT MISSING THAT SHE'D PASSED OVER.
SHE WAS WILD. ACTING OUT BECAUSE SHE COULD. BUT ONCE I SOBERED UP, SHE STARTED TO COME AROUND.
IT WAS GOOD OF SYBIL TO PAY YOU TO FIND MY TEENIE.
HOLY BIBLE

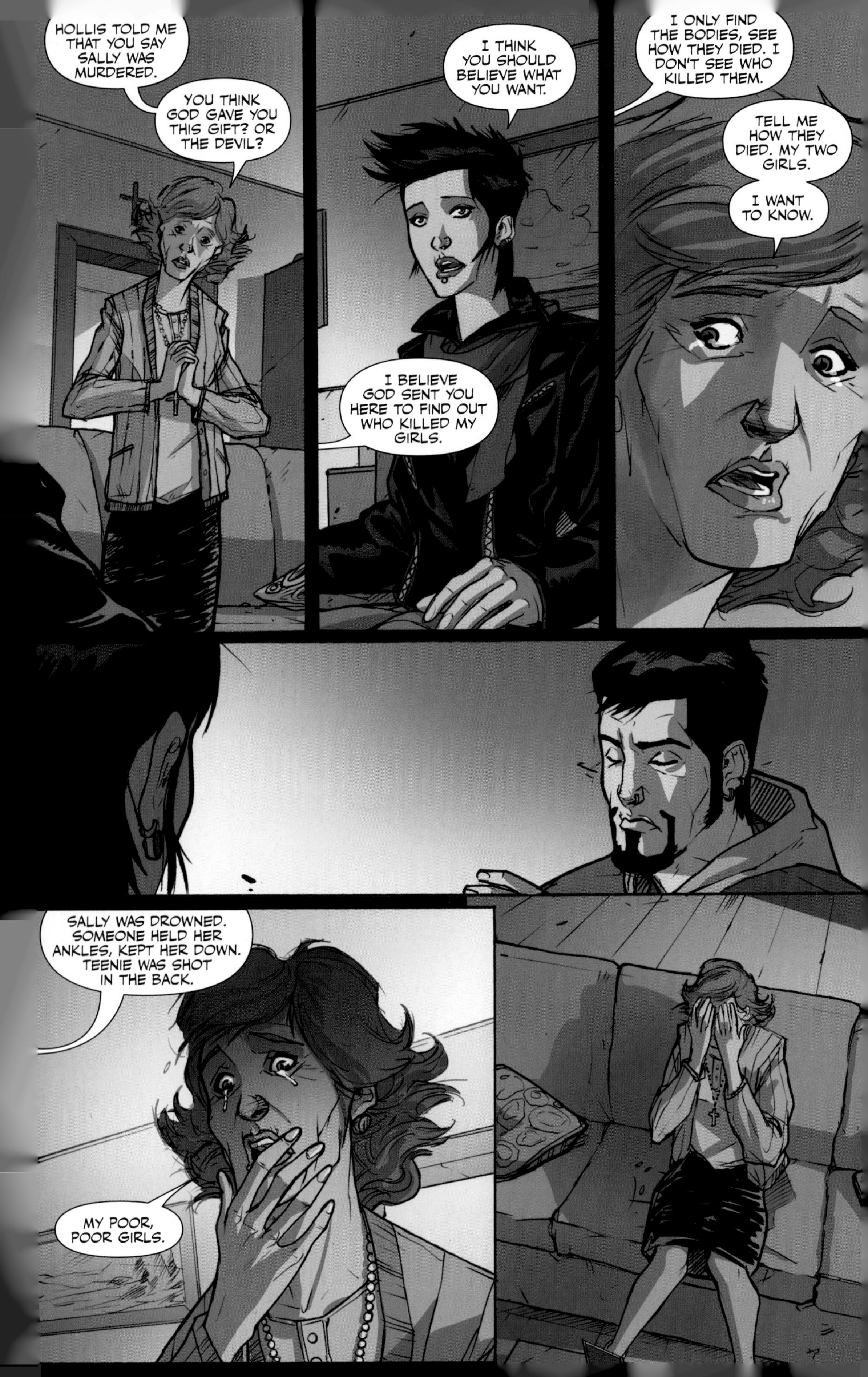
HOLLIS TOLD ME THAT YOU SAY SALLY WAS MURDERED.
YOU THINK GOD GAVE YOU THIS GIFT? OR THE DEVIL?
I THINK YOU SHOULD BELIEVE WHAT YOU WANT.
I BELIEVE GOD SENT YOU HERE TO FIND OUT WHO KILLED MY GIRLS.
I ONLY FIND THE BODIES, SEE HOW THEY DIED. I DON'T SEE WHO KILLED THEM.
TELL ME HOW THEY DIED. MY TWO GIRLS.
I WANT TO KNOW.
SALLY WAS DROWNED. SOMEONE HELD HER ANKLES, KEPT HER DOWN. TEENIE WAS SHOT IN THE BACK.
MY POOR, POOR GIRLS.

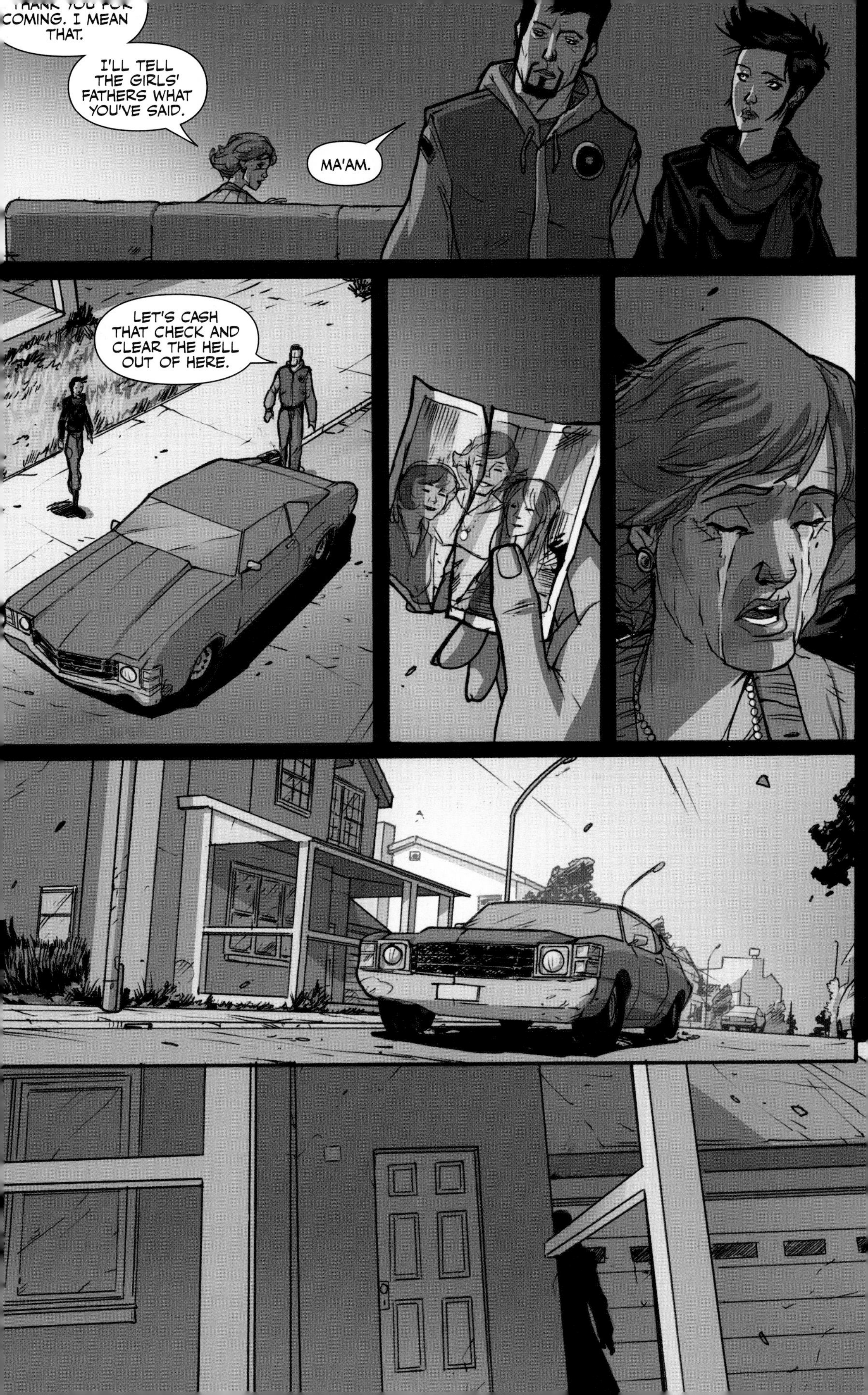
THANK YOU FOR COMING. I MEAN THAT.
I'LL TELL THE GIRLS' FATHERS WHAT YOU'VE SAID.
MA'AM.
LET'S CASH THAT CHECK AND CLEAR THE HELL OUT OF HERE.

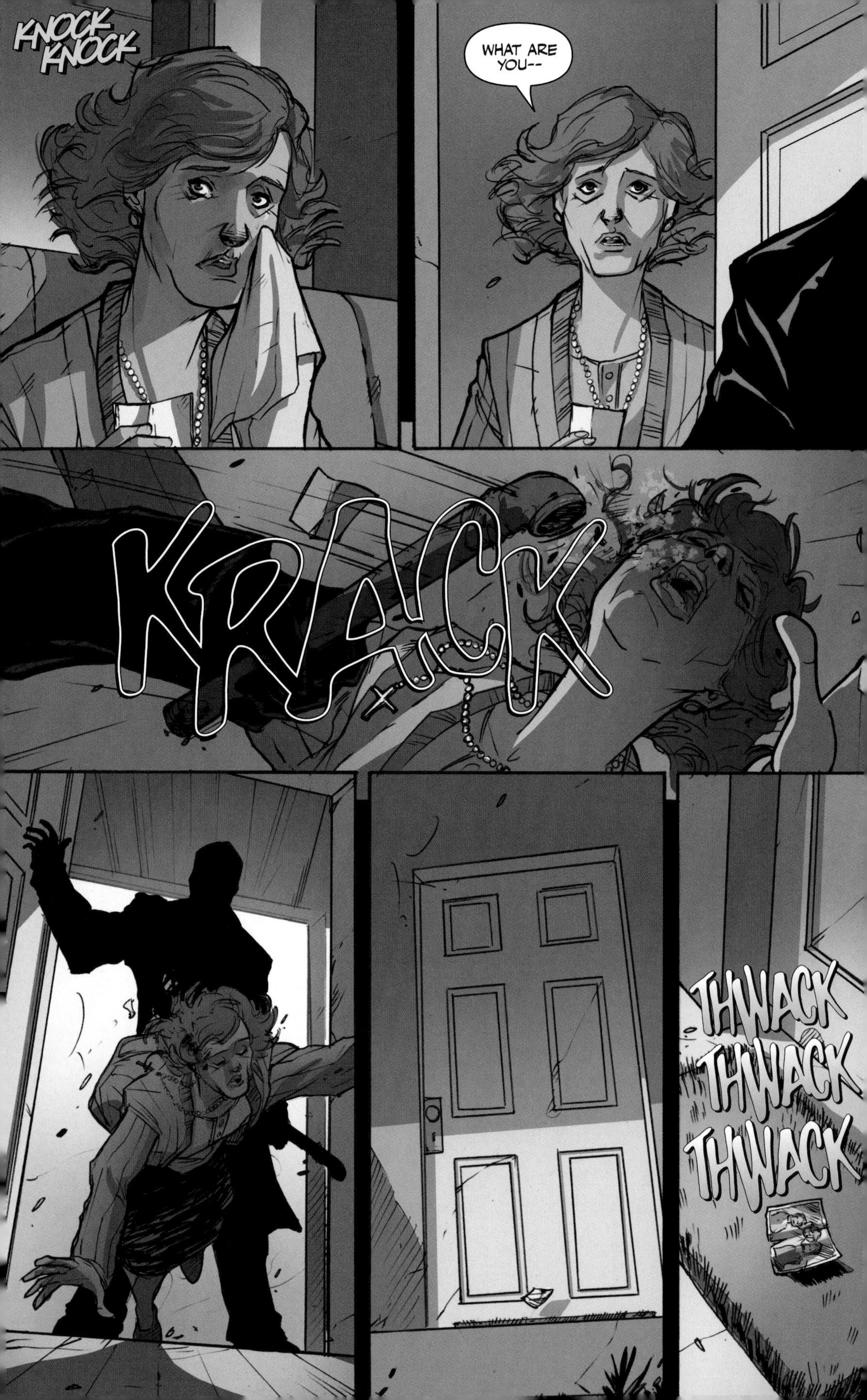
KNOCK KNOCK
WHAT ARE YOU--
KRACK
THWACK THWACK THWACK

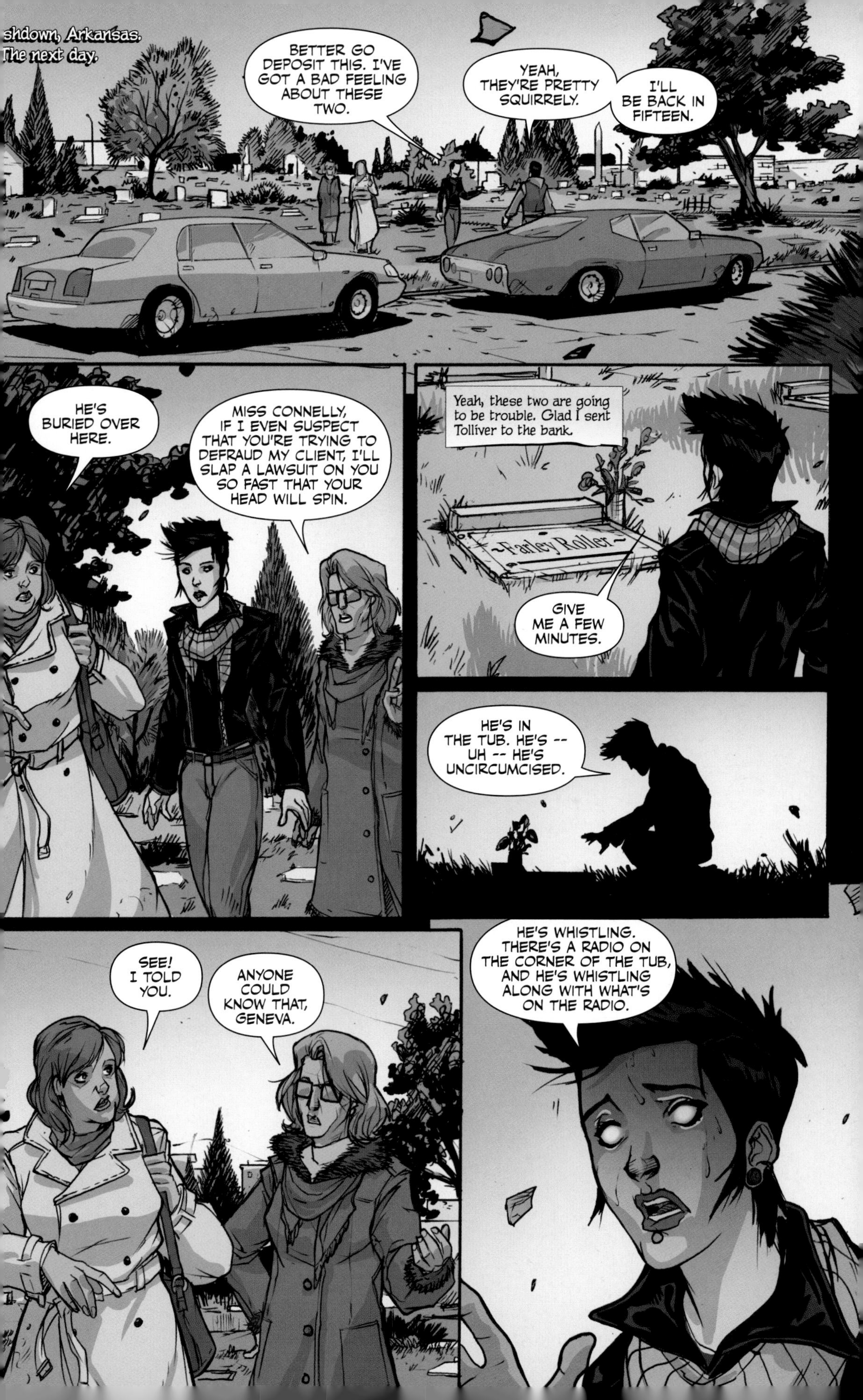
shdown, Arkansas.
The next day.
BETTER GO DEPOSIT THIS. I'VE GOT A BAD FEELING ABOUT THESE TWO.
YEAH, THEY'RE PRETTY SQUIRRELY.
I'LL BE BACK IN FIFTEEN.
HE'S BURIED OVER HERE.
MISS CONNELLY, IF I EVEN SUSPECT THAT YOU'RE TRYING TO DEFRAUD MY CLIENT, I'LL SLAP A LAWSUIT ON YOU SO FAST THAT YOUR HEAD WILL SPIN.
Yeah, these two are going to be trouble. Glad I sent Tolliver to the bank.
~Farley Roller~
GIVE ME A FEW MINUTES.
HE'S IN THE TUB. HE'S -- UH -- HE'S UNCIRCUMCISED.
SEE! I TOLD YOU.
ANYONE COULD KNOW THAT, GENEVA.
HE'S WHISTLING. THERE'S A RADIO ON THE CORNER OF THE TUB, AND HE'S WHISTLING ALONG WITH WHAT'S ON THE RADIO.

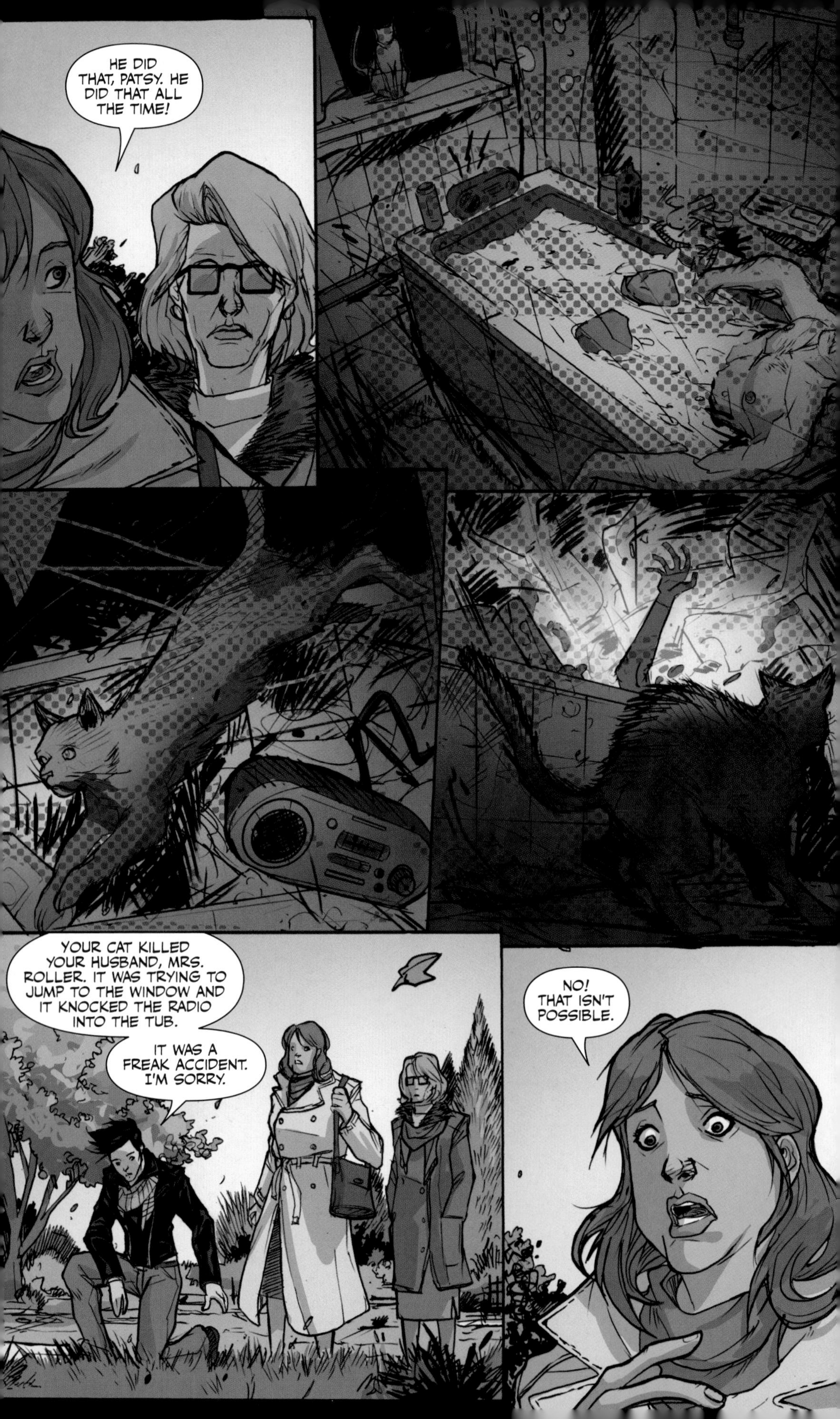
HE DID THAT, PATSY. HE DID THAT ALL THE TIME!
YOUR CAT KILLED YOUR HUSBAND, MRS. ROLLER. IT WAS TRYING TO JUMP TO THE WINDOW AND IT KNOCKED THE RADIO INTO THE TUB.
IT WAS A FREAK ACCIDENT. I'M SORRY.
NO! THAT ISN'T POSSIBLE.

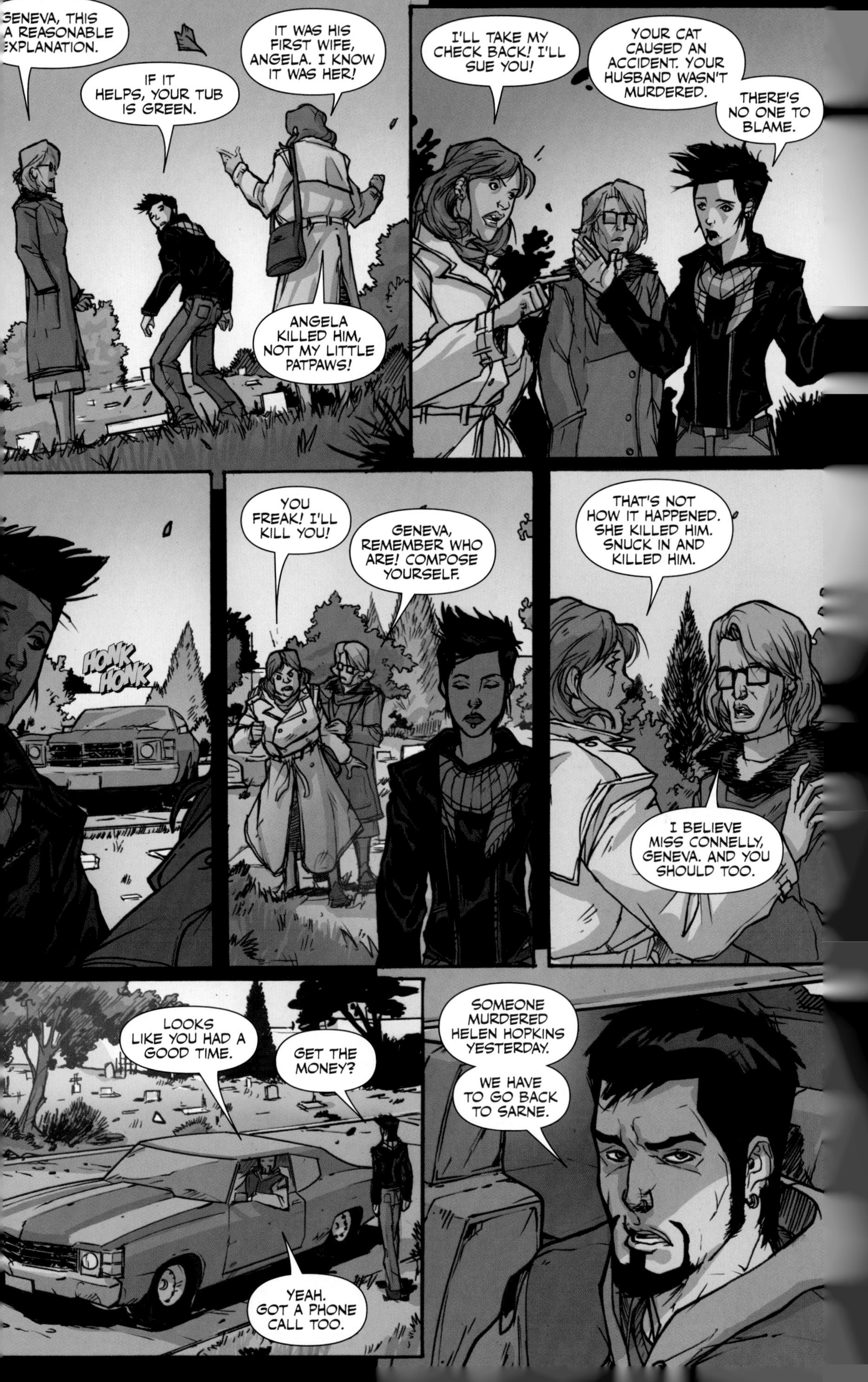
GENEVA, THIS A REASONABLE EXPLANATION.
IF IT HELPS, YOUR TUB IS GREEN.
IT WAS HIS FIRST WIFE, ANGELA. I KNOW IT WAS HER!
ANGELA KILLED HIM, NOT MY LITTLE PATPAWS!
I'LL TAKE MY CHECK BACK! I'LL SUE YOU!
YOUR CAT CAUSED AN ACCIDENT. YOUR HUSBAND WASN'T MURDERED.
THERE'S NO ONE TO BLAME.
HONK HONK
YOU FREAK! I'LL KILL YOU!
GENEVA, REMEMBER WHO ARE! COMPOSE YOURSELF.
THAT'S NOT HOW IT HAPPENED. SHE KILLED HIM. SNUCK IN AND KILLED HIM.
I BELIEVE MISS CONNELLY, GENEVA. AND YOU SHOULD TOO.
LOOKS LIKE YOU HAD A GOOD TIME.
GET THE MONEY?
YEAH. GOT A PHONE CALL TOO.
SOMEONE MURDERED HELEN HOPKINS YESTERDAY.
WE HAVE TO GO BACK TO SARNE.

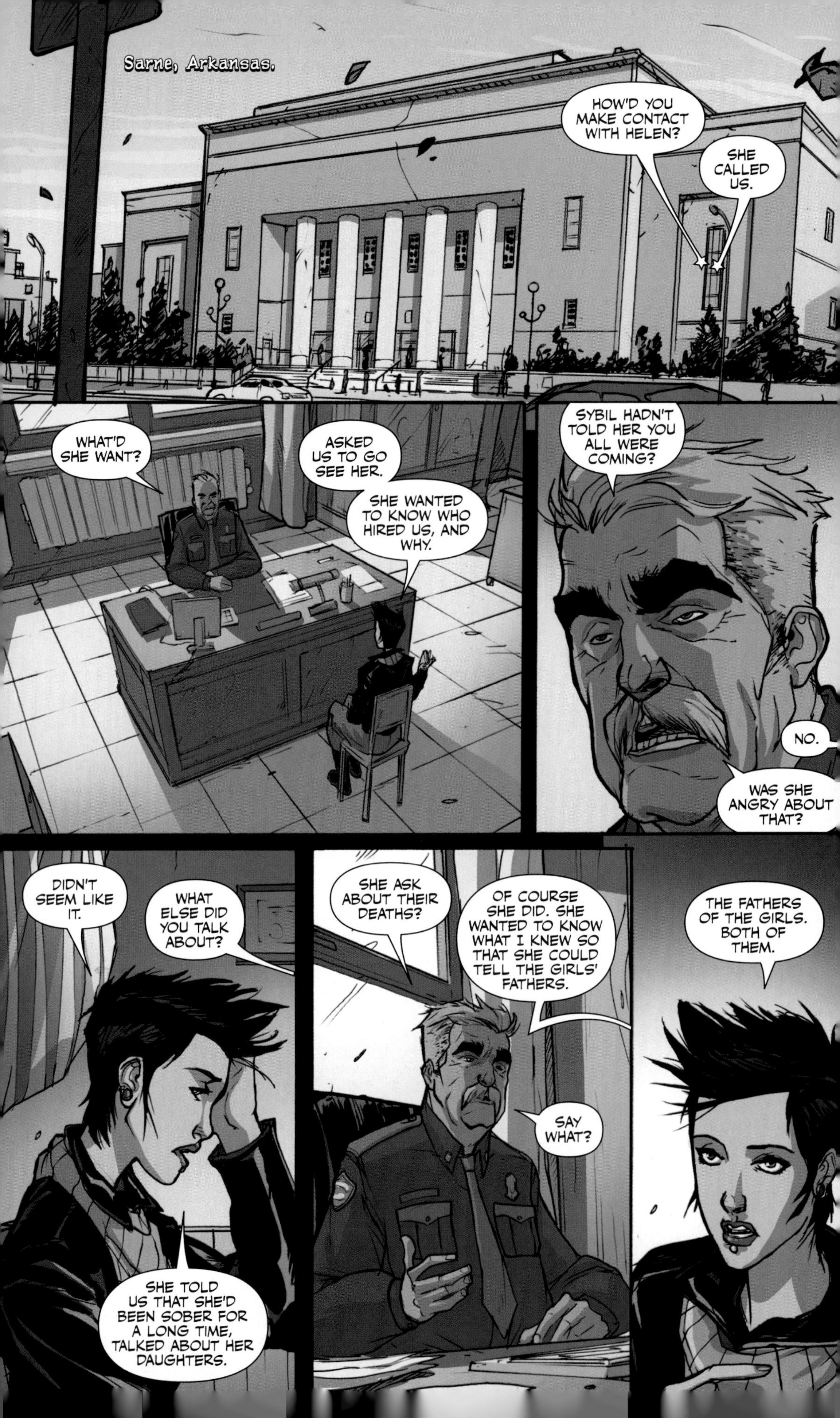

Sarne, Arkansas.
HOW'D YOU MAKE CONTACT WITH HELEN?
SHE CALLED US.
WHAT'D SHE WANT?
ASKED US TO GO SEE HER.
SHE WANTED TO KNOW WHO HIRED US, AND WHY.
SYBIL HADN'T TOLD HER YOU ALL WERE COMING?
NO.
WAS SHE ANGRY ABOUT THAT?
DIDN'T SEEM LIKE IT.
WHAT ELSE DID YOU TALK ABOUT?
SHE TOLD US THAT SHE'D BEEN SOBER FOR A LONG TIME, TALKED ABOUT HER DAUGHTERS.
SHE ASK ABOUT THEIR DEATHS?
OF COURSE SHE DID. SHE WANTED TO KNOW WHAT I KNEW SO THAT SHE COULD TELL THE GIRLS' FATHERS.
SAY WHAT?
THE FATHERS OF THE GIRLS. BOTH OF THEM.

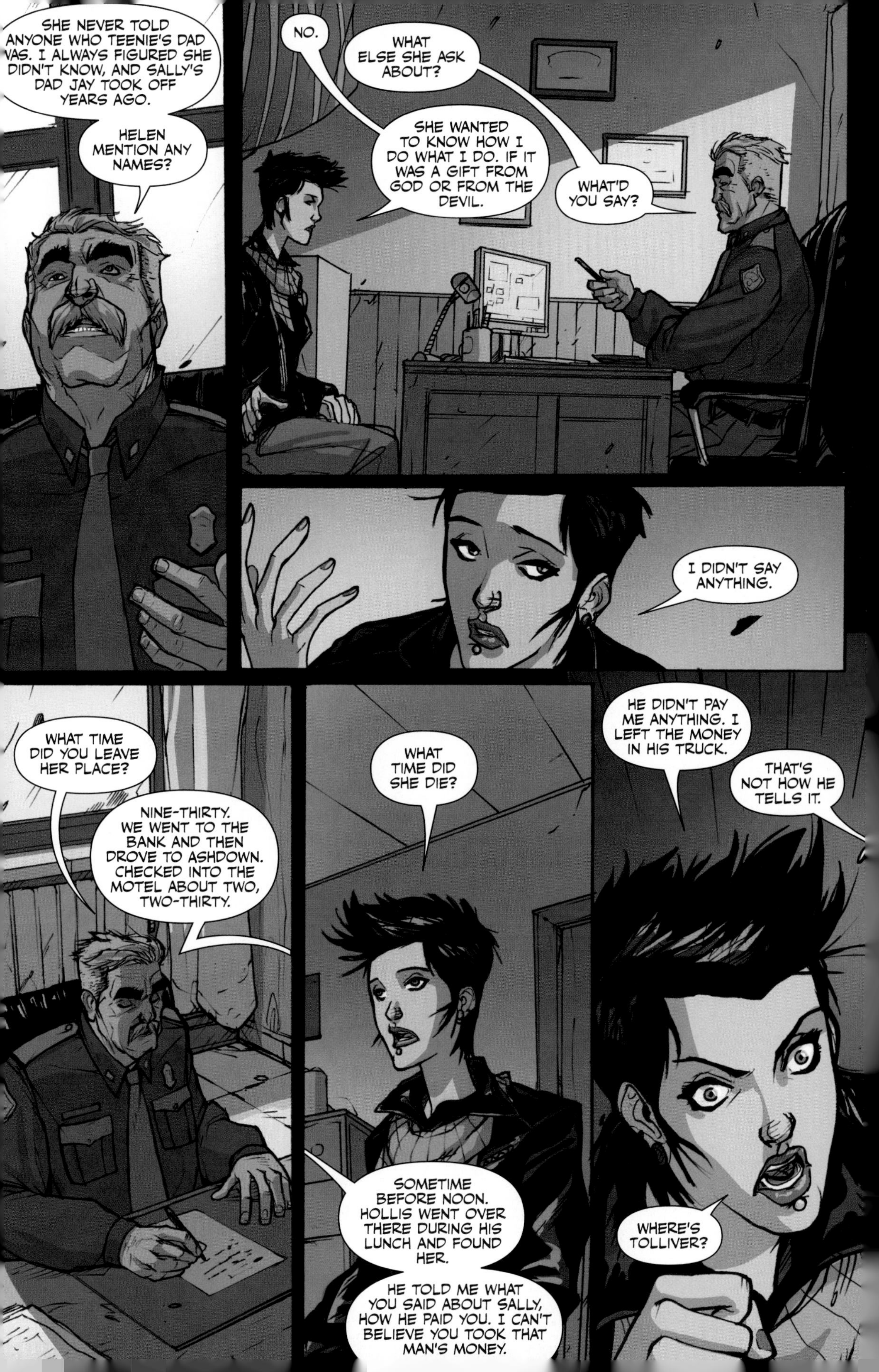
SHE NEVER TOLD ANYONE WHO TEENIE'S DAD VAS. I ALWAYS FIGURED SHE DIDN'T KNOW, AND SALLY'S DAD JAY TOOK OFF YEARS AGO.
HELEN MENTION ANY NAMES?
NO.
WHAT ELSE SHE ASK ABOUT?
SHE WANTED TO KNOW HOW I DO WHAT I DO. IF IT WAS A GIFT FROM GOD OR FROM THE DEVIL.
WHAT'D YOU SAY?
I DIDN'T SAY ANYTHING.
WHAT TIME DID YOU LEAVE HER PLACE?
NINE-THIRTY. WE WENT TO THE BANK AND THEN DROVE TO ASHDOWN. CHECKED INTO THE MOTEL ABOUT TWO, TWO-THIRTY.
WHAT TIME DID SHE DIE?
SOMETIME BEFORE NOON. HOLLIS WENT OVER THERE DURING HIS LUNCH AND FOUND HER.
HE TOLD ME WHAT YOU SAID ABOUT SALLY, HOW HE PAID YOU. I CAN'T BELIEVE YOU TOOK THAT MAN'S MONEY.
HE DIDN'T PAY ME ANYTHING. I LEFT THE MONEY IN HIS TRUCK.
THAT'S NOT HOW HE TELLS IT.
WHERE'S TOLLIVER?

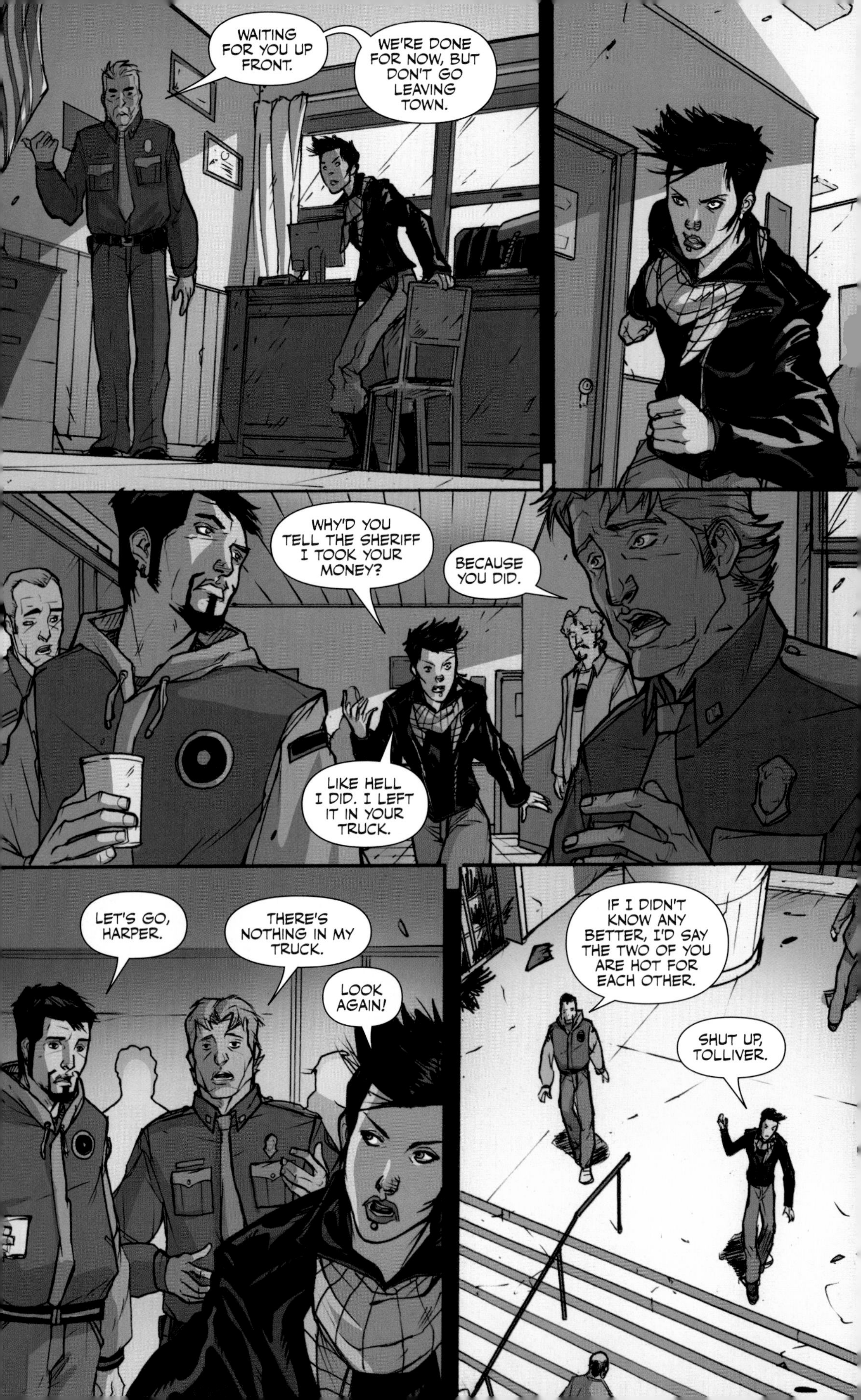
WAITING FOR YOU UP FRONT.
WE'RE DONE FOR NOW, BUT DON'T GO LEAVING TOWN.
WHY'D YOU TELL THE SHERIFF I TOOK YOUR MONEY?
BECAUSE YOU DID.
LIKE HELL I DID. I LEFT IT IN YOUR TRUCK.
LET'S GO, HARPER.
THERE'S NOTHING IN MY TRUCK.
LOOK AGAIN!
IF I DIDN'T KNOW ANY BETTER, I'D SAY THE TWO OF YOU ARE HOT FOR EACH OTHER.
SHUT UP, TOLLIVER.

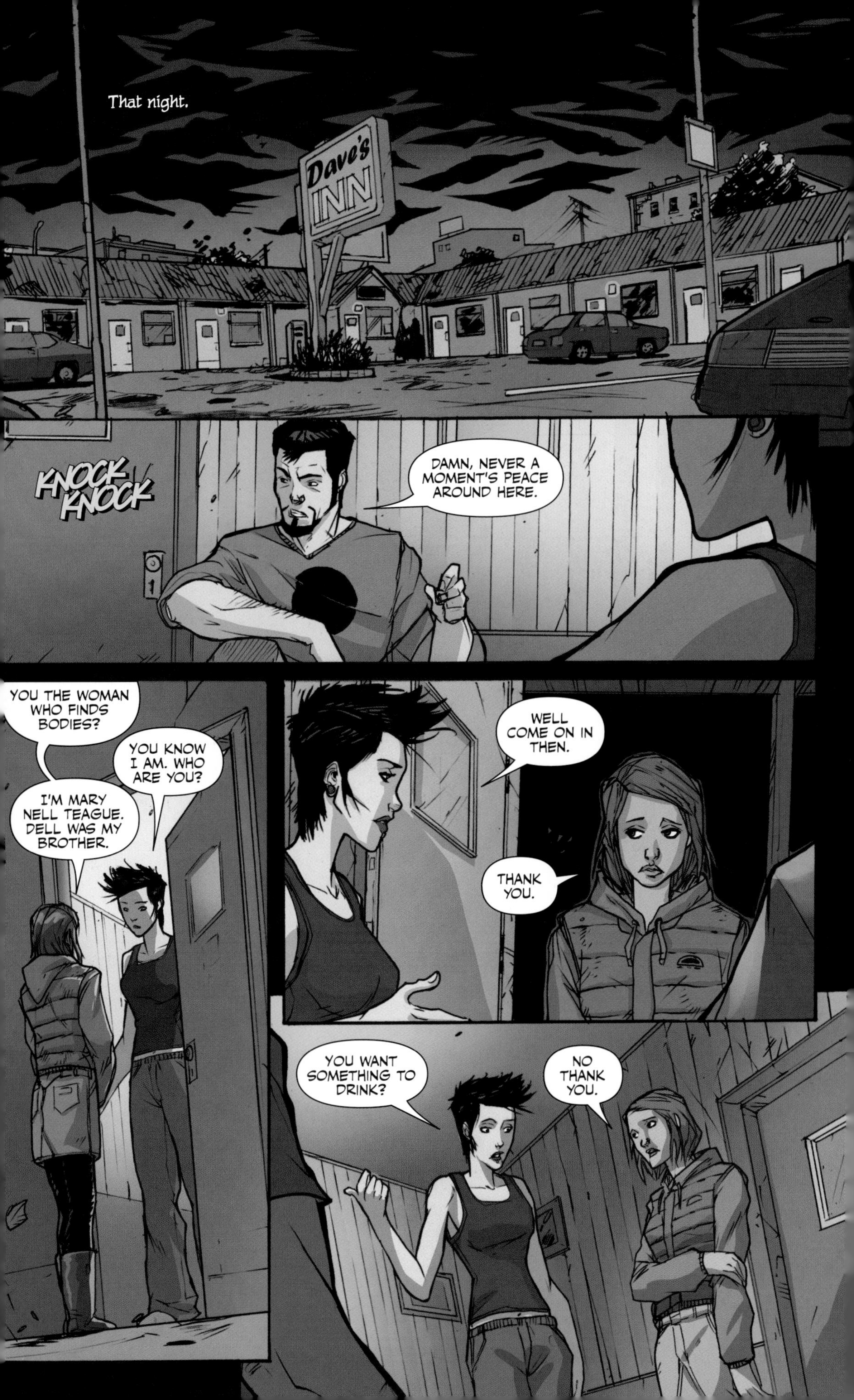
That night.
Dave's INN
KNOCK KNOCK
DAMN, NEVER A MOMENT'S PEACE AROUND HERE.
YOU THE WOMAN WHO FINDS BODIES?
YOU KNOW I AM. WHO ARE YOU?
I'M MARY NELL TEAGUE. DELL WAS MY BROTHER.
WELL COME ON IN THEN.
THANK YOU.
YOU WANT SOMETHING TO DRINK?
NO THANK YOU.

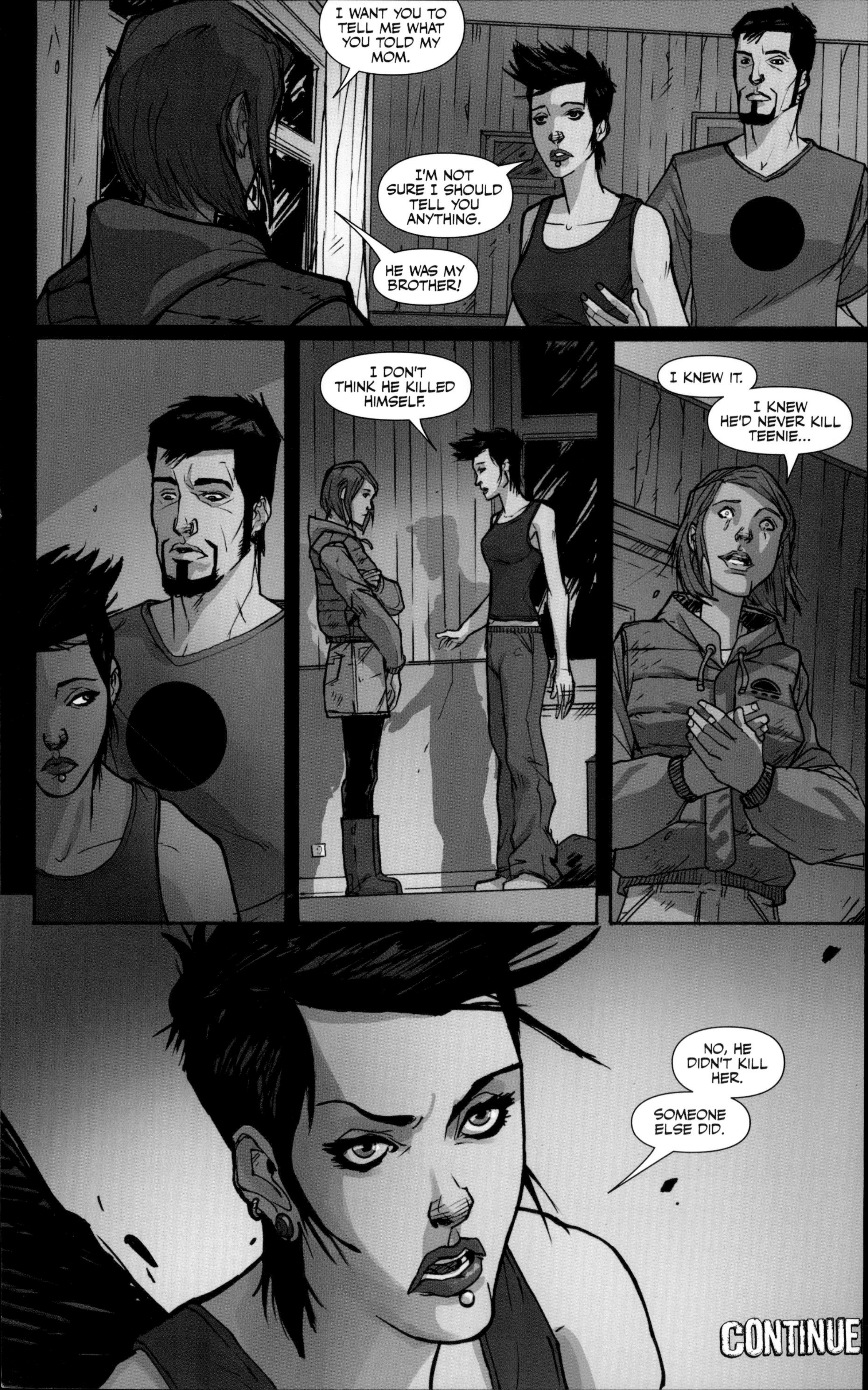
I WANT YOU TO TELL ME WHAT YOU TOLD MY MOM.
I'M NOT SURE I SHOULD TELL YOU ANYTHING.
HE WAS MY BROTHER!
I DON'T THINK HE KILLED HIMSELF.
I KNEW IT.
I KNEW HE'D NEVER KILL TEENIE...
NO, HE DIDN'T KILL HER.
SOMEONE ELSE DID.
CONTINUE

GRAVE SIGHT
BONUS MATERIAL

THE MAKING OF GRAVE SIGHT
A LOOK AT THE GRAPHIC NOVEL PROCESS FROM SCRIPT TO COLORS

CHARLAINE HARRIS' GRAVE SIGHT # 1

PAGE FIFTEEN

PANEL 1: Establishing shot of the deep woods, on the side of a hill. Harper's wearing large, dark sunglasses, a red scarf, blue padded jacket, gloves, and hiking boots. Tolliver's dressed in the same type of clothing. Hollis, in deputy uniform, stands next to them.

This is the Ozarks, so the ground should be covered with leaves, trees are everywhere, and here and there the bald faces of rocks are exposed, jutting up out of the ground.

CAPTION: Two hours later.

HOLLIS: This is where they found Dell's body.

HARPER: What happened to him?

HOLLIS: Shot twice in the head. One shot grazed the skull, the other entered through the eye.

PANEL 2: Harper's not buying this. She looks at Hollis.

HARPER: Two shots? Where'd you find the gun?

HOLLIS: Didn't.

HARPER: That seems like something of a problem.

PANEL 3: On Hollis. Be sure to show the name tag on his jacket: Hollis Boxleitner.

HOLLIS: Someone could've stolen it. Guns are expensive.

PANEL 4: Harper starts to walk away from the site. In the foreground, Tolliver sends Hollis on his way.

TOLLIVER: Okay, we'll take it from here.

HOLLIS: Shouldn't I come with you?

TOLLIVER: We need anything, we'll holler.

PANEL 5: Wide-angle shot. Harper and Tolliver walk one way, Hollis the other.

PANEL 6: On Harper and Tolliver.

HARPER: They can't really believe that Dell killed himself. Shot twice, and no gun?

TOLLIVER: Yeah, that's some bullshit. Wonder what they're not telling us.

HARPER: The sooner I find her, the sooner this isn't our problem.

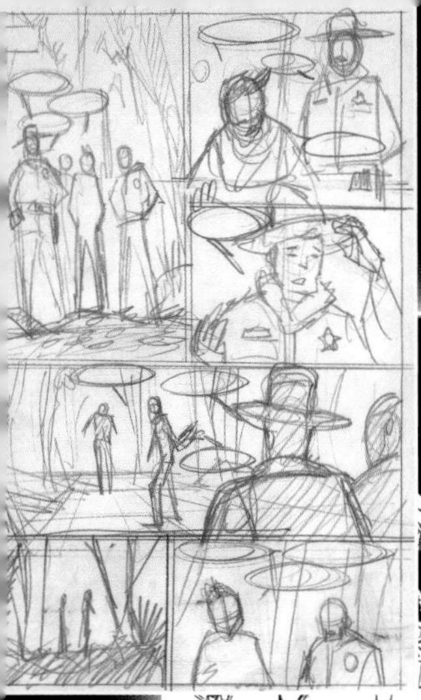

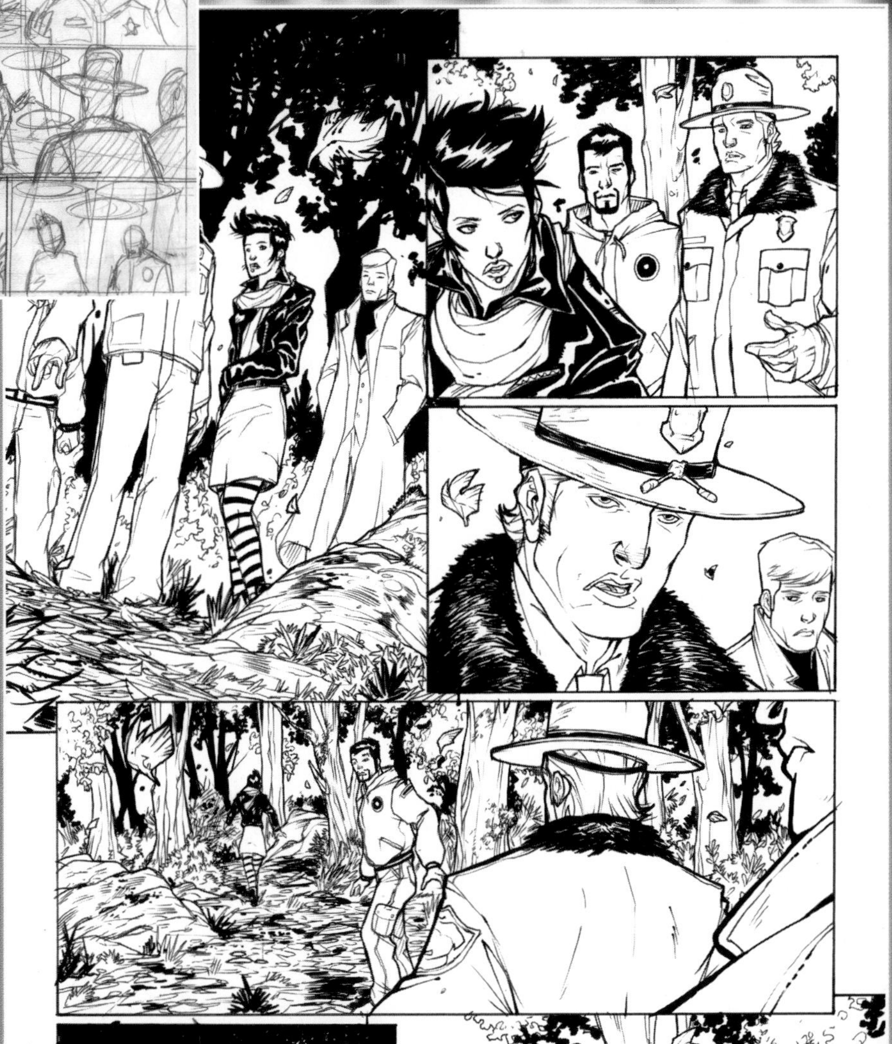

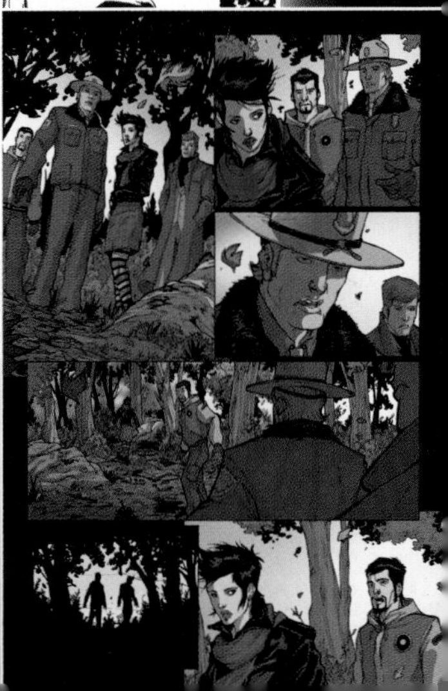

Top: rough layout by DENIS MEDRI
Center: final pencils and inks by DENIS MEDRI
Bottom: final colors by PAOLO FRANCESCUTTO

CHARLAINE HARRIS' GRAVE SIGHT # 1

PAGE SIXTEEN

PANEL 1: Harper and Tolliver move through the woods, Harper leading the way.

PANEL 2: Harper's head suddenly jerks in one direction.

TOLLIVER (OP): You feel something?

HARPER: Yeah. This way.

PANEL 3: They continue up the hill, walking silently, Harper "feeling" her way.

PANEL 4: Still on the hill. The area's clear of trees, and Harper's kneeling down, hands hovering above a pile of dry, dead branches and leaves.

PANEL 5: Tight on Harper's eyes. We see them through the glasses — her eyes have gone totally white, are wide open as she experiences the last moments of Teenie's life.

PANEL 6: Same, but now Harper's eyes are morphing into a new scene: Teenie (teenager, pretty but poor) running through the woods at night.

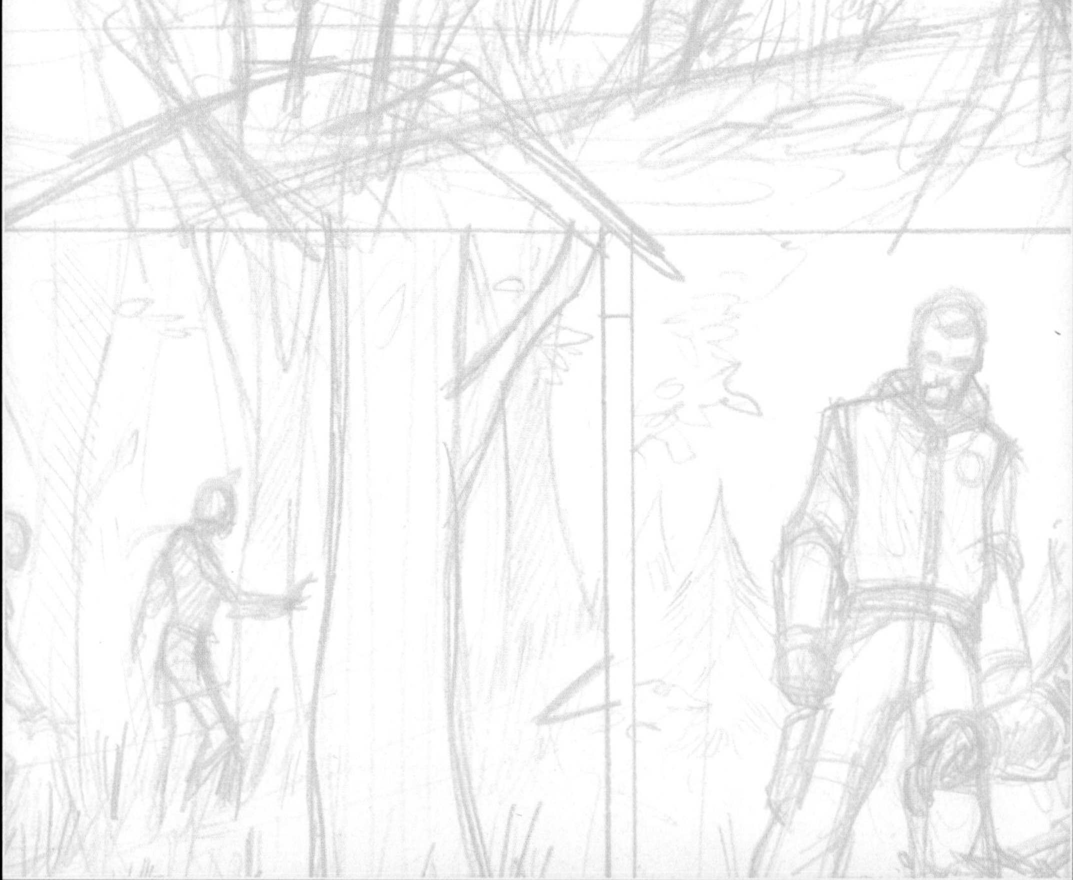

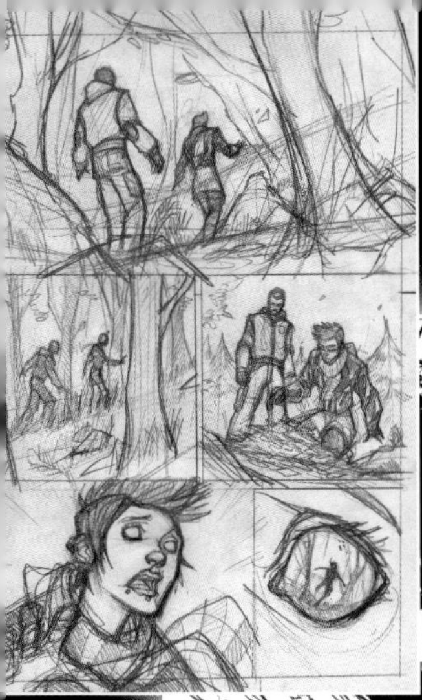

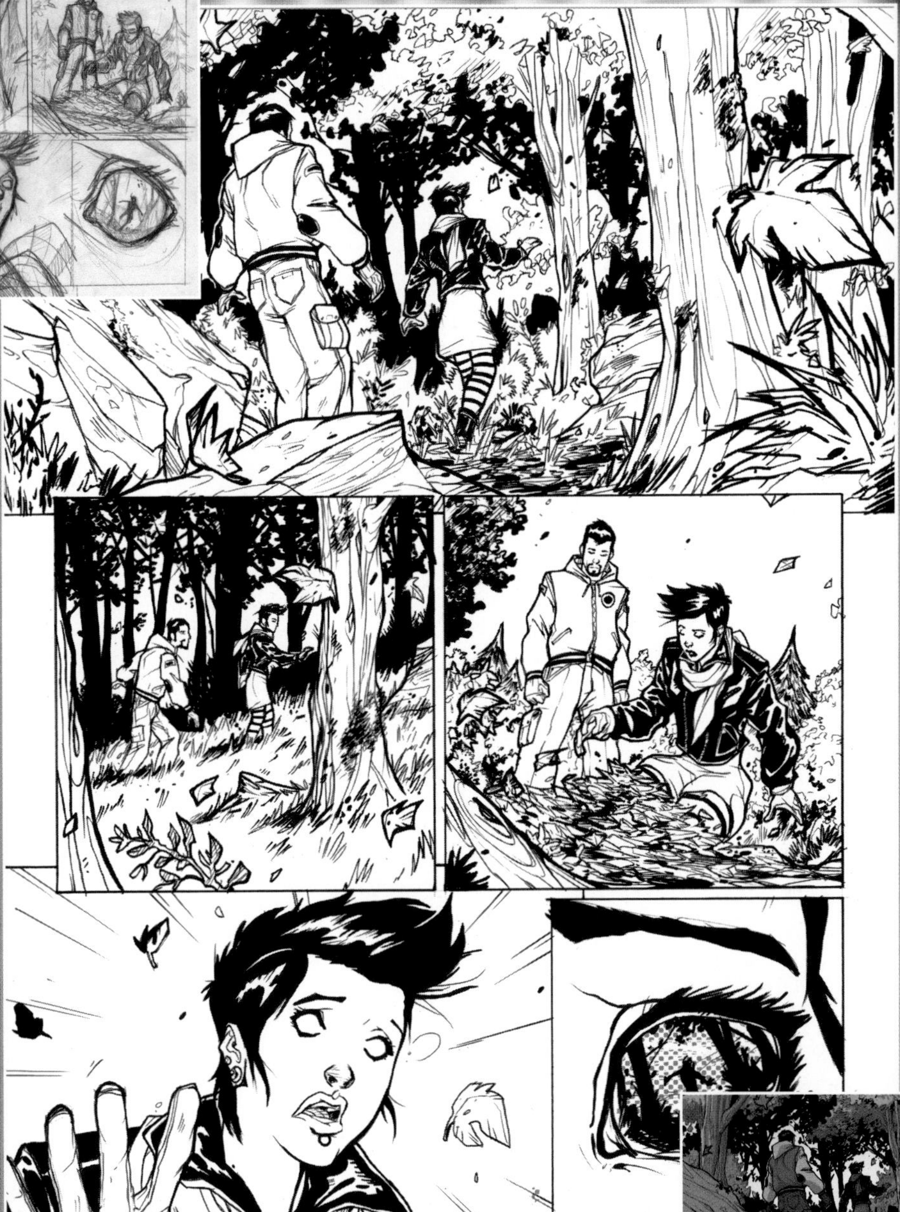

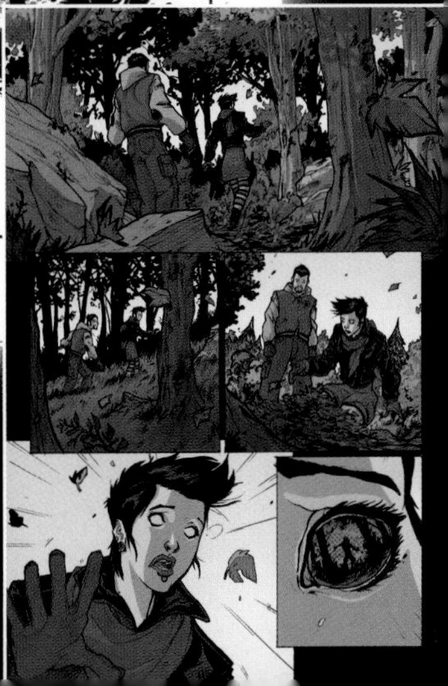

Top: rough layout by DENIS MEDRI
Center: final pencils and inks by DENIS MEDRI
Bottom: final colors by PAOLO FRANCESCUTTO

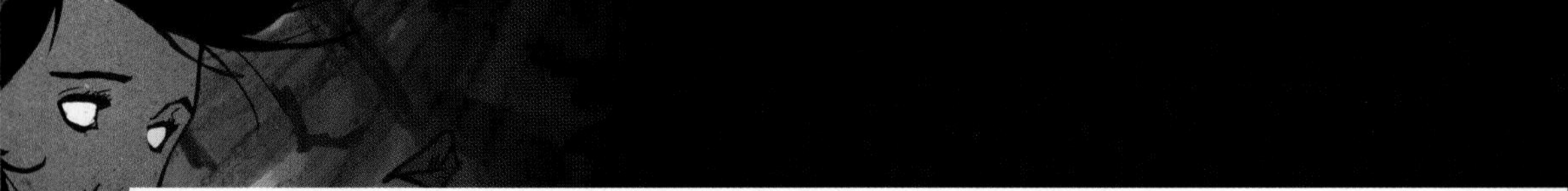

CHARLAINE HARRIS' GRAVE SIGHT # 1

PAGE SEVENTEEN

PANEL 1: We're now "seeing" the last moments of Teenie's life the same way Harper's sees it, through her powers. This is a weird flashback, everything angled and exaggerated. Teenie continues to run, starting up the same hill, panting and terrified.

TEENIE (weird, dream-like): …oh God…

PANEL 2: Tight on Teenie. She looks back over her shoulder, scared out of his mind.

TEENIE (weird, dream-like): …please, leave me alone…

PANEL 3: Teenie struggles up the hill, trying to run but having a hard time getting traction, keeping her balance. This is a wide, pulled back shot. Really show how small Teenie is in comparison to the world around her.

PANEL 4: Wide panel. Teenie, small in the panel, is shot in the back.

SFX: BLAM

PANEL 5: Teenie on her stomach, hands digging into the cold earth. Blood pooling out from her mouth, from the wound in her back. She's dying.

PANEL 6: On the ground, near Teenie's face, looking up. A shadowed figure stands behind her, gun pointed down. The gun fires, once again striking her in the back.

SFX: BLAM

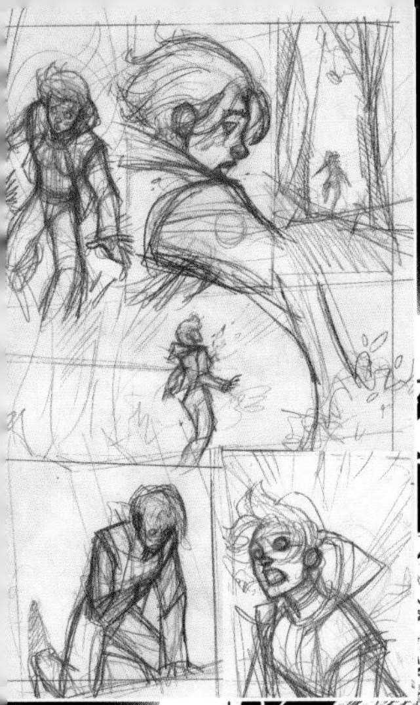

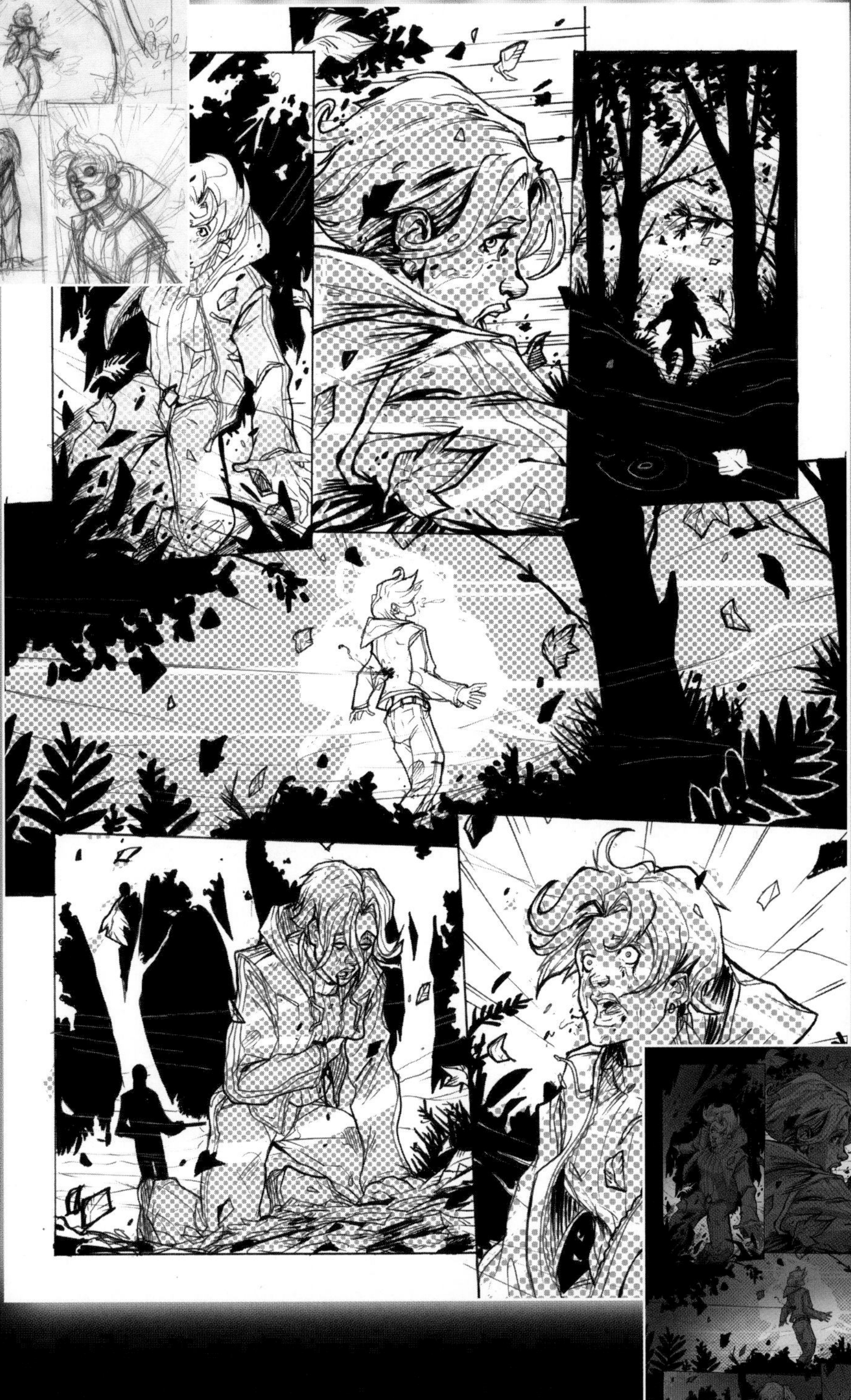

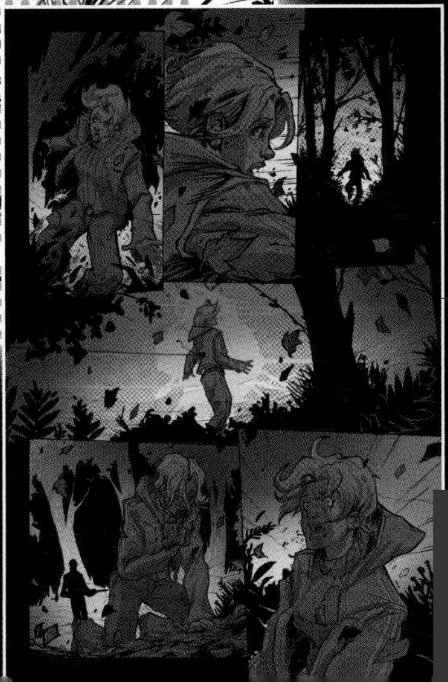

Top: rough layout by DENIS MEDRI
Center: final pencils and inks by DENIS MEDRI
Bottom: final colors by PAOLO FRANCESCUTTO

CHARLAINE HARRIS' GRAVE SIGHT # 1

PAGE EIGHTEEN

PANEL 1: Harper's on her hands and knees, fists holding clumps of earth and leaves. Tolliver stands next to her, trying to help her up.

TOLLIVER: You all right?

HARPER (weak): She was shot twice, in the back.

HARPER (weak): She was running as fast as she could, trying so hard to escape.

PANEL 2: Tolliver helps Harper to her feet.

TOLLIVER: C'mon, let's get you back to the truck.

PANEL 3: The two of them walk through the woods, heading back the way they'd come.

PANEL 4: Another shot of them walking through the woods.

PANEL 5: They emerge from the woods. The woods go right up to a small road; parked on the side of the road is an SUV belong to the Sheriff's department. Hollis and Edwards stand near the SUV. Both are alarmed at the appearance of Harper and Tolliver.

TOLLIVER: She needs a Coke.

TOLLIVER: Now.

EDWARDS: Did she find Teenie?

PANEL 6: Tight on Harper. The glasses off, her eyes empty and cold. She's drained, physically and emotionally.

HARPER: Of course I found her.

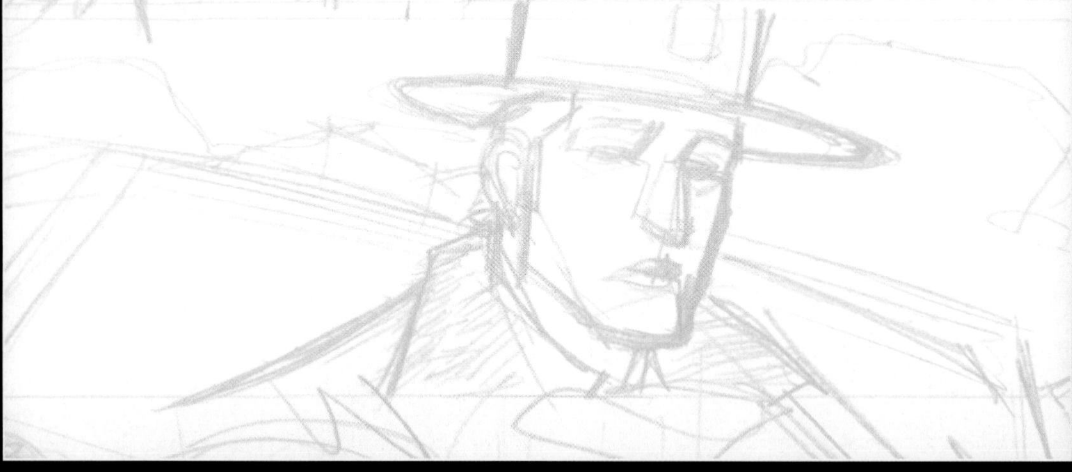

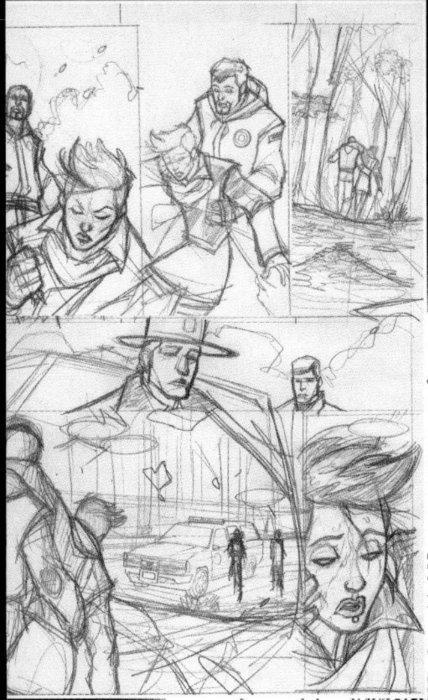

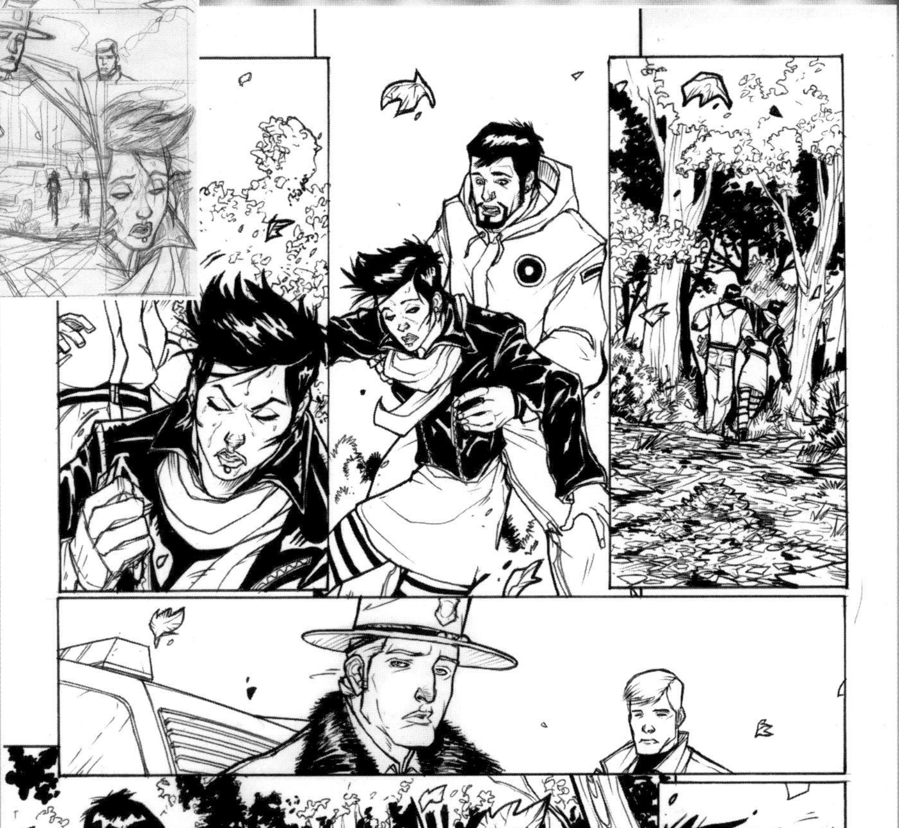

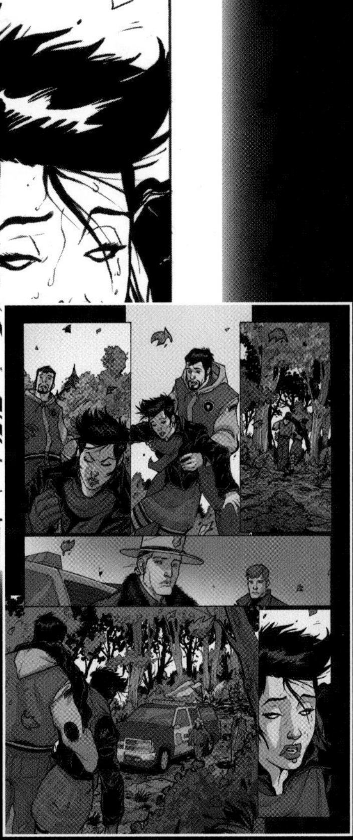

Top: rough layout by DENIS MEDRI
Center: final pencils and inks by DENIS MEDRI
Bottom: final colors by PAOLO FRANCESCUTTO

CHARLAINE HARRIS' GRAVE SIGHT # 1

PAGE NINETEEN

PANEL 1: Establishing shot of the hotel where Harper and Tolliver are staying. Their car is parked out front.

> *HARPER CAPTION: Tolliver decided to head back down to the diner, pay a visit to that waitress.

> *HARPER CAPTION: He tried to be clever about it, but I'm his sister. He can't hide things like that from me.

PANEL 2: The TV blares in the background, and Harper looks down at a folder that's open in front of her. Clippings from newspapers and magazines are scattered around the bed. All have headlines that pertain to Cameron's disappearance.

> HEADLINE: NO TRACE OF CAMERON CONNELLY

> HEADLINE: INVESTIGATORS CLAIM NO LEADS HAVE BEEN FOUND

> HEADLINES: THE MYSTERIOUS DISAPPEARANCE OF CAMERON CONNELLY

PANEL 3: There's a knock at the door and Harper walks toward the door.

> SFX: KNOCK KNOCK

> HARPER: One second.

PANEL 4: Harper stands in the open doorway. Hollis stands on the other side of the door, still in his uniform.

> HARPER: Deputy Boxleitner?

> HOLLIS: Call me Hollis.

> HARPER: Did you confirm the identity of the body I found?

PANEL 5: Hollis, nervous, doesn't want to be here, seen with Harper.

> HOLLIS: No, we're still waiting for the dental records. Probably won't get them until some time tomorrow.

> HARPER (OP): Which means Tolliver and I have to stick around a bit longer.

> HOLLIS: That's right. Listen, that's not why I came here.

PANEL 6: Hollis gestures for Harper to come outside.

> HOLLIS: You want to go for a drive?

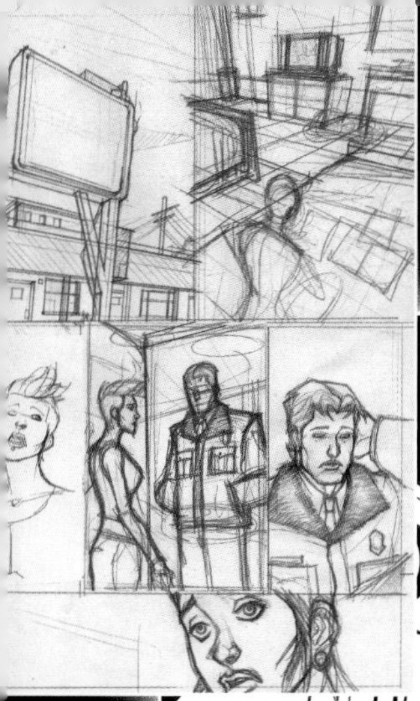

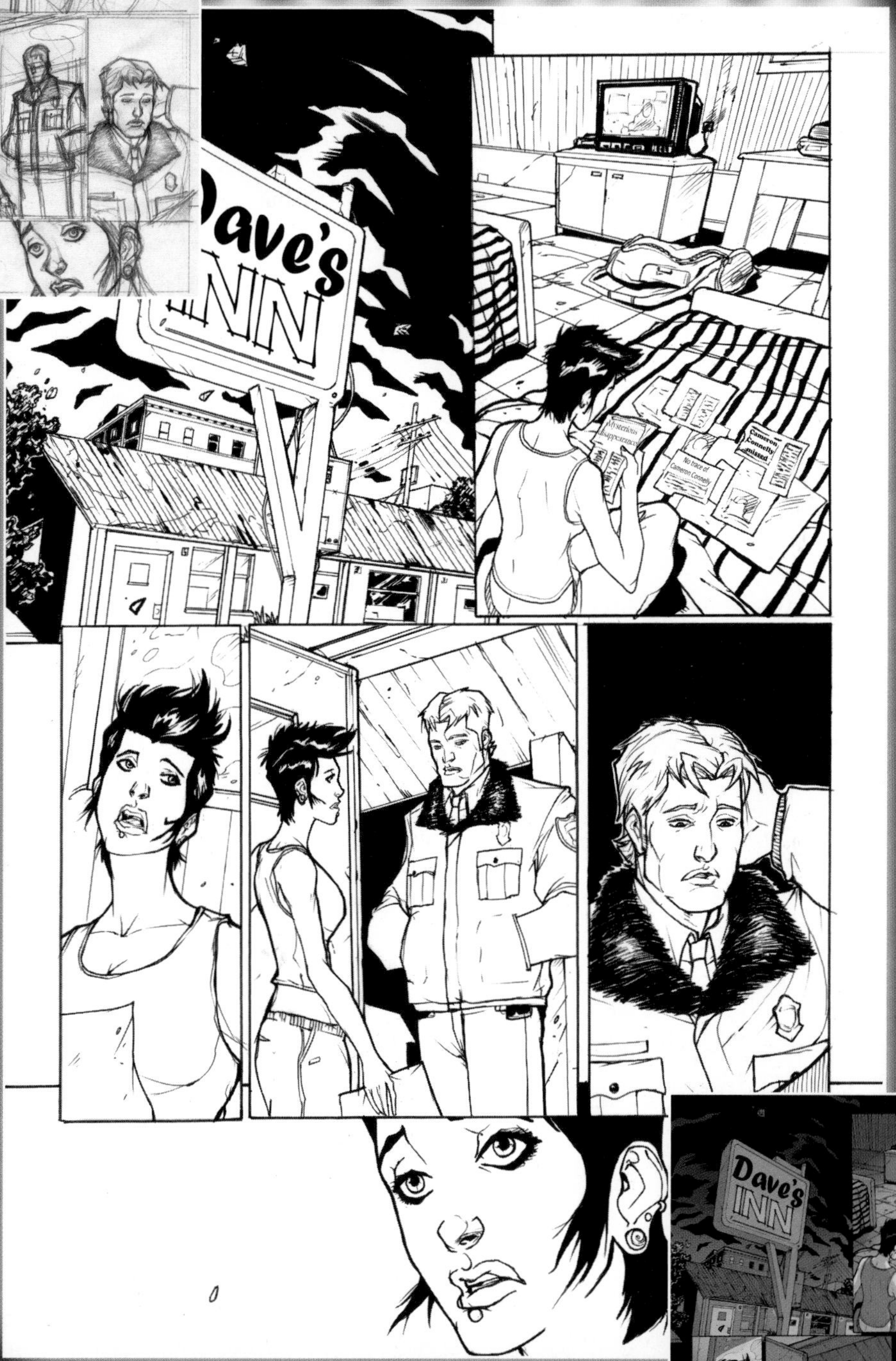
Dave's
INN
Mysterious disappearance
No trace of Cameron Connelly
Cameron Connelly missed

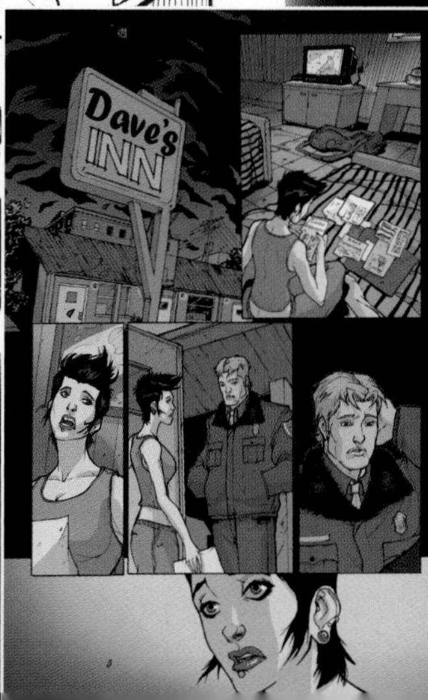
Dave's
INN

Top: rough layout by DENIS MEDRI
Center: final pencils and inks by DENIS MEDRI
Bottom: final colors by PAOLO FRANCESCUTTO

CHARLAINE HARRIS' GRAVE SIGHT # 1

PAGE TWENTY

PANEL 1: Establishing shot of Hollis' blue truck driving through Sarne.

    HOLLIS CAPTION: "Did you know that Teenie was my sister-in-law?"

    HARPER CAPTION: "No. Through marriage?"

    HOLLIS CAPTION: "Was married to her sister, Sally."

PANEL 2: Inside of the truck. Harper and Hollis drink milk shakes from Sonic.

    HARPER: Was? You get divorced?

    HOLLIS: She died.

    HARPER: I'm sorry.

    HARPER: I am too.

PANEL 3: The two of them eat their shakes, and Harper looks at Hollis.

PANEL 4: On Harper. She's had enough of this.

    HARPER: What do you, want Hollis?

PANEL 5: Hollis stares straight ahead, out the windshield.

    HOLLIS: How … how do people hire you?

PANEL 6: On Harper. So that's what all of this is about.

    HARPER: They pay me money and I do what they ask.

    HOLLIS (OP): How much?

    HARPER: Depends. Usually around five thousand dollars.

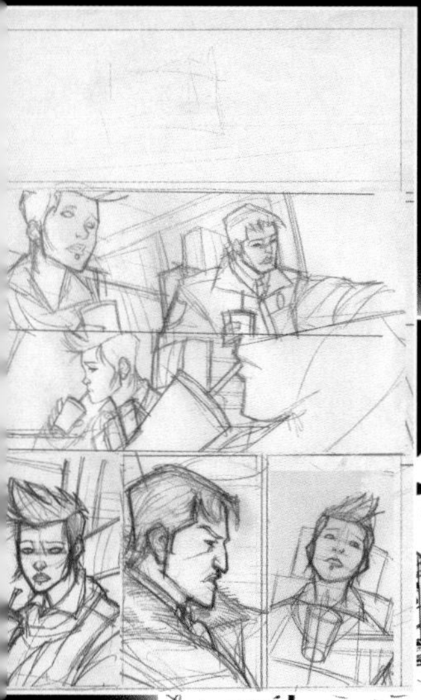

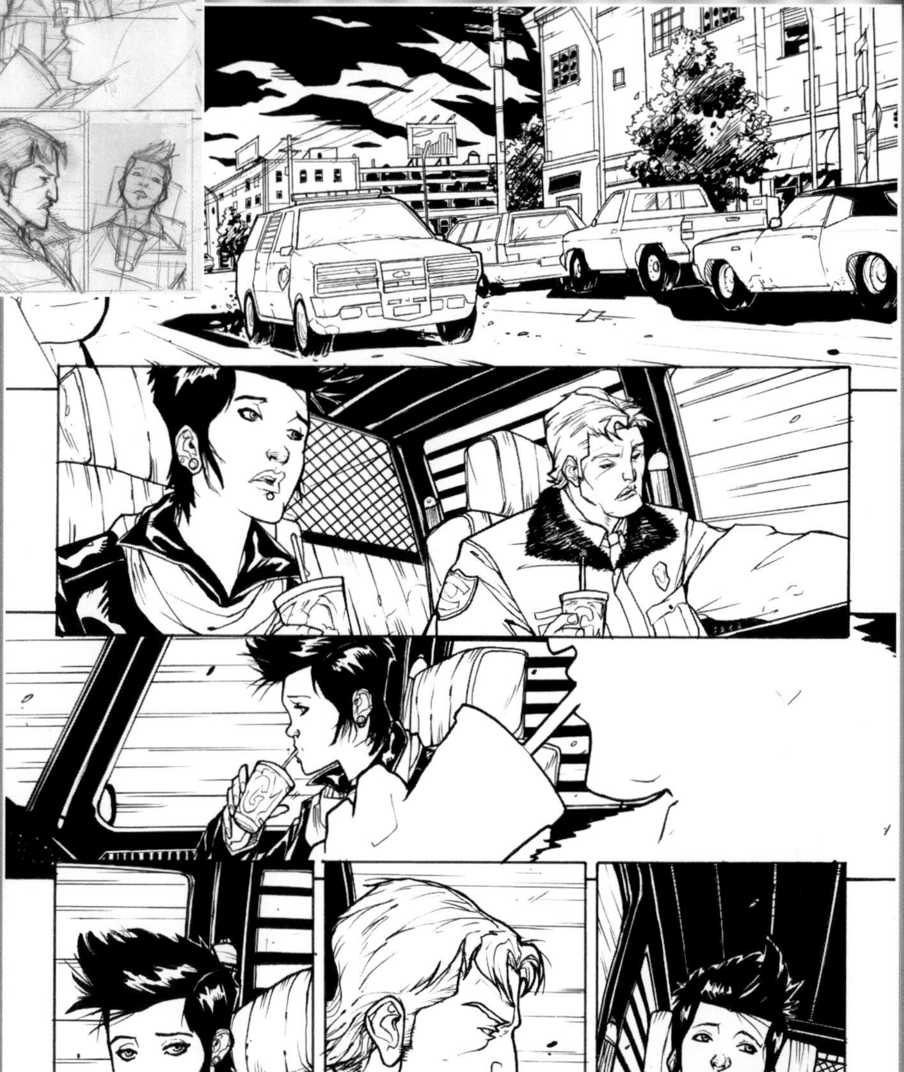

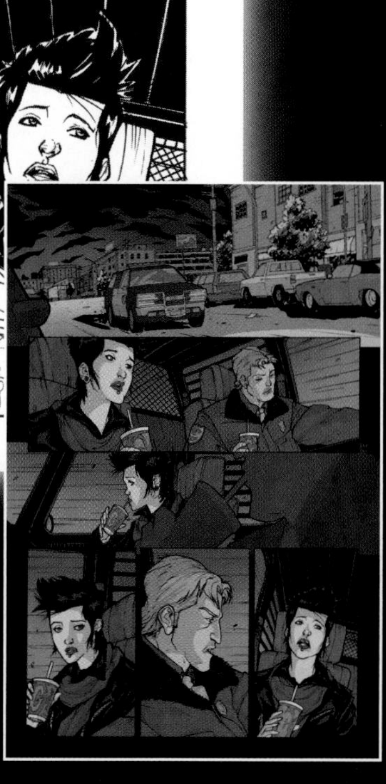

Top: rough layout by DENIS MEDRI
Center: final pencils and inks by DENIS MEDRI
Bottom: final colors by PAOLO FRANCESCUTTO

CHARLAINE HARRIS' GRAVE SIGHT # 1

PAGE TWENTY-ONE

PANEL 1: Hollis holds an envelope of money in front of him. Still looking straight ahead.

HOLLIS: Looks like I guessed low.

HOLLIS: This is three thousand. It's all I have.

PANEL 2: Harper takes the envelope.

HARPER: What do you want to find out?

PANEL 3: Hollis finally looks at Harper.

HOLLIS: How my wife died.

PANEL 4: The truck backs out of the stall at the Sonic.

HARPER CAPTION: "Where is she?"

HOLLIS CAPTION: "Not far."

PANEL 5: The truck drives down a lonely, winding road.

PANEL 6: The truck stops in front of a cemetery. Harper and Hollis are getting out.

HOLLIS: Over here.

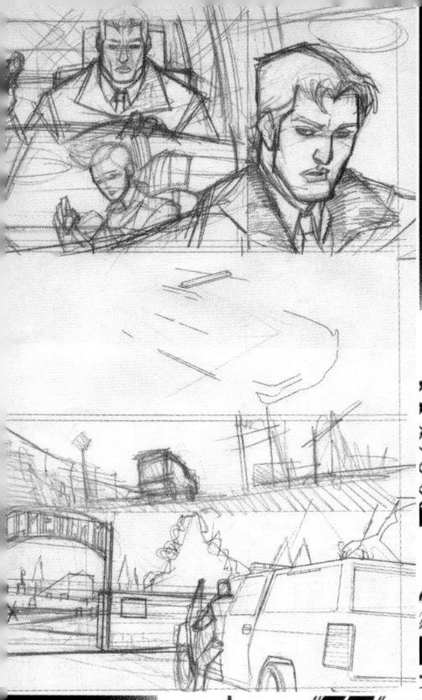

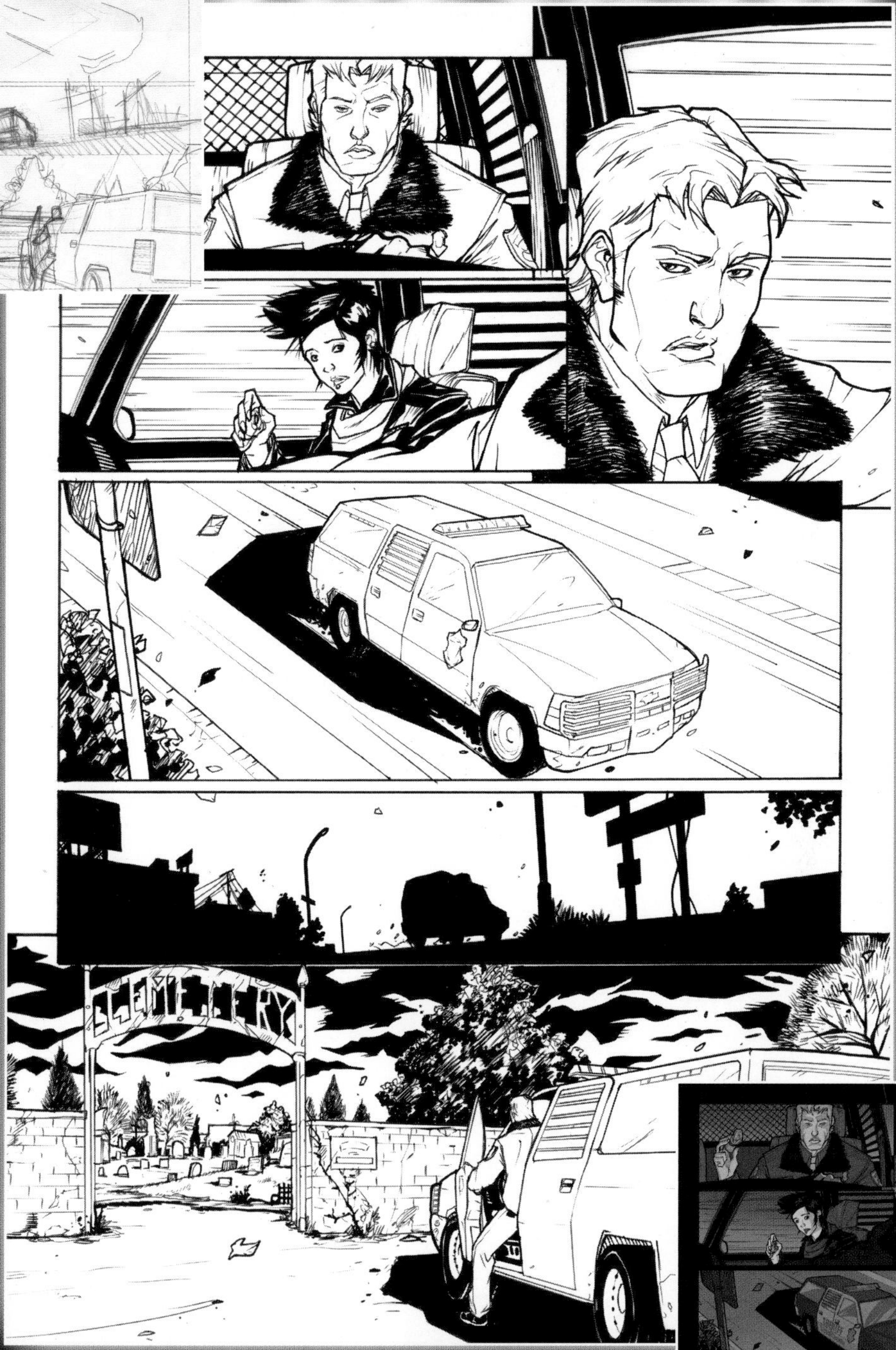
CEMETERY

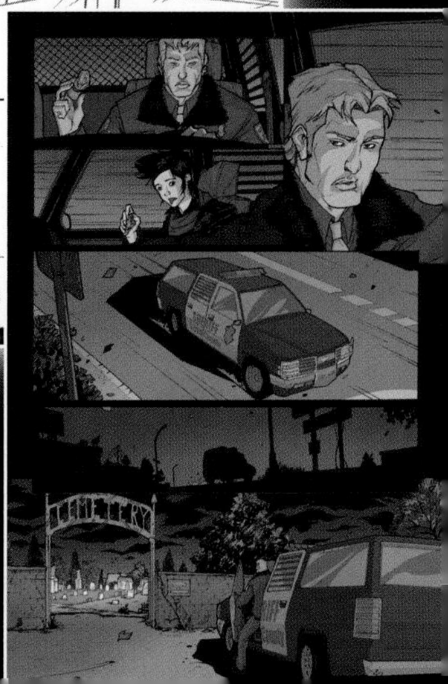

Top: rough layout by DENIS MEDRI
Center: final pencils and inks by DENIS MEDRI
Bottom: final colors by PAOLO FRANCESCUTTO

CHARLAINE HARRIS' GRAVE SIGHT # 1

PAGE TWENTY-TWO

PANEL 1: Harper stands near a grave, hands outstretched, eyes closed.

PANEL 2: Through Harper's vision: Sally's face is visible, underwater, gasping for breath, eyes wide open with terror.

PANEL 3: Tight on the bathtub where Sally drowned. She's under the water, her feet jutting up out of the tub. Two gloved hands hold her ankles. Sally thrashes, but it's not doing any good.

PANEL 4: Back in the cemetery. Harper's weak, down on her knees.

HARPER (weak): She drowned…

HOLLIS (OP): I know. But what *happened*?

PANEL 5: Rest of the page. Harper looks at Hollis, her face drained and empty.

HARPER: Someone killed her. Held her by the ankles, kept her under until she was dead.

CAPTION: Continued.

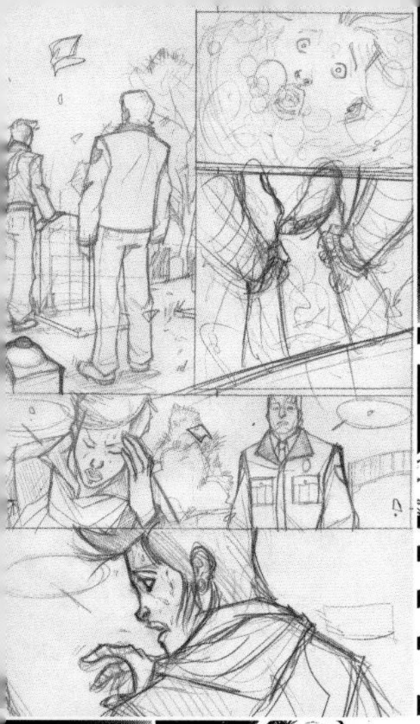

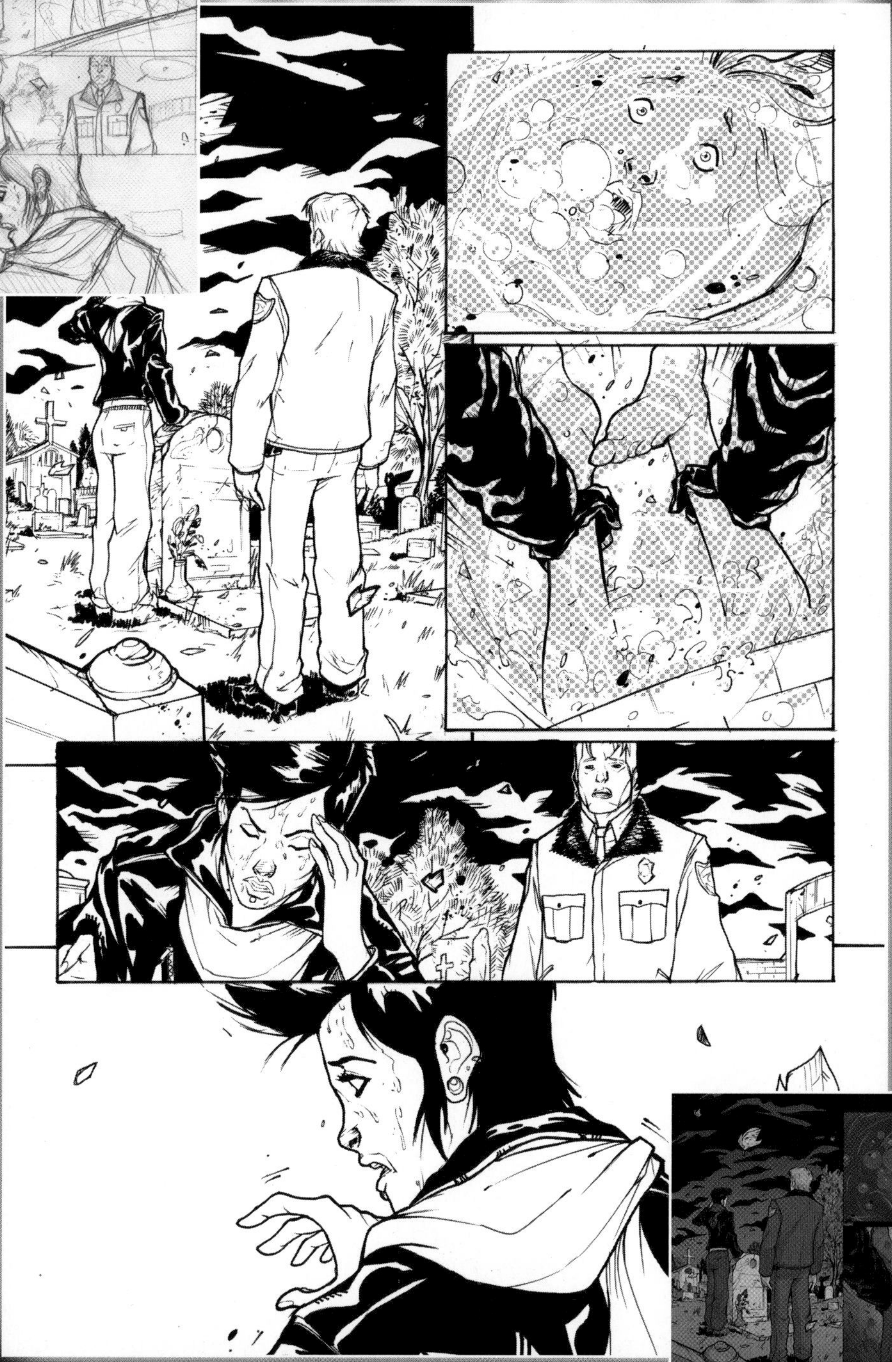

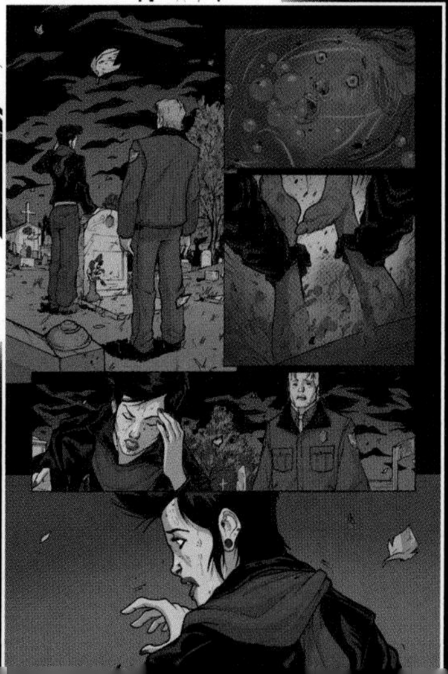

Top: rough layout by DENIS MEDRI
Center: final pencils and inks by DENIS MEDRI
Bottom: final colors by PAOLO FRANCESCUTTO

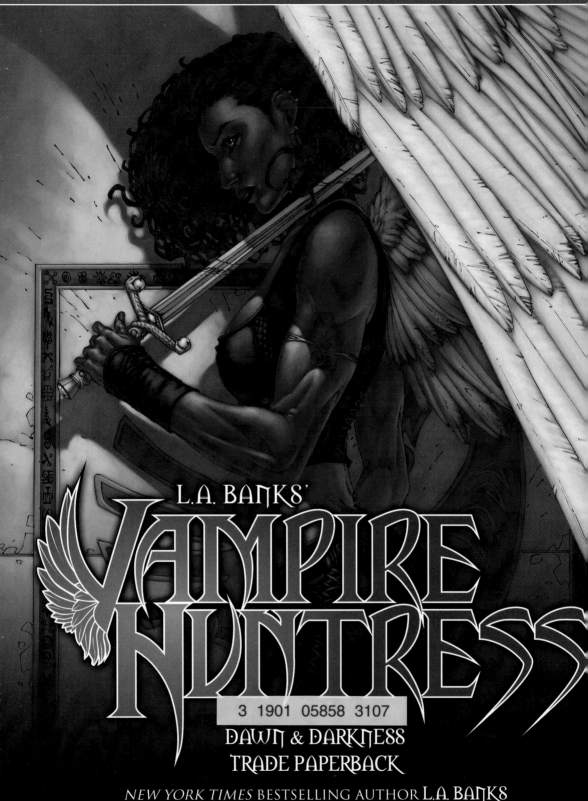